DISCOVER YOUR
INNER
PSYCHIC

DISCOVER YOUR
INNER
PSYCHIC

Focus your energies to gain better understanding of yourself and others

TARA WARD

ARCTURUS

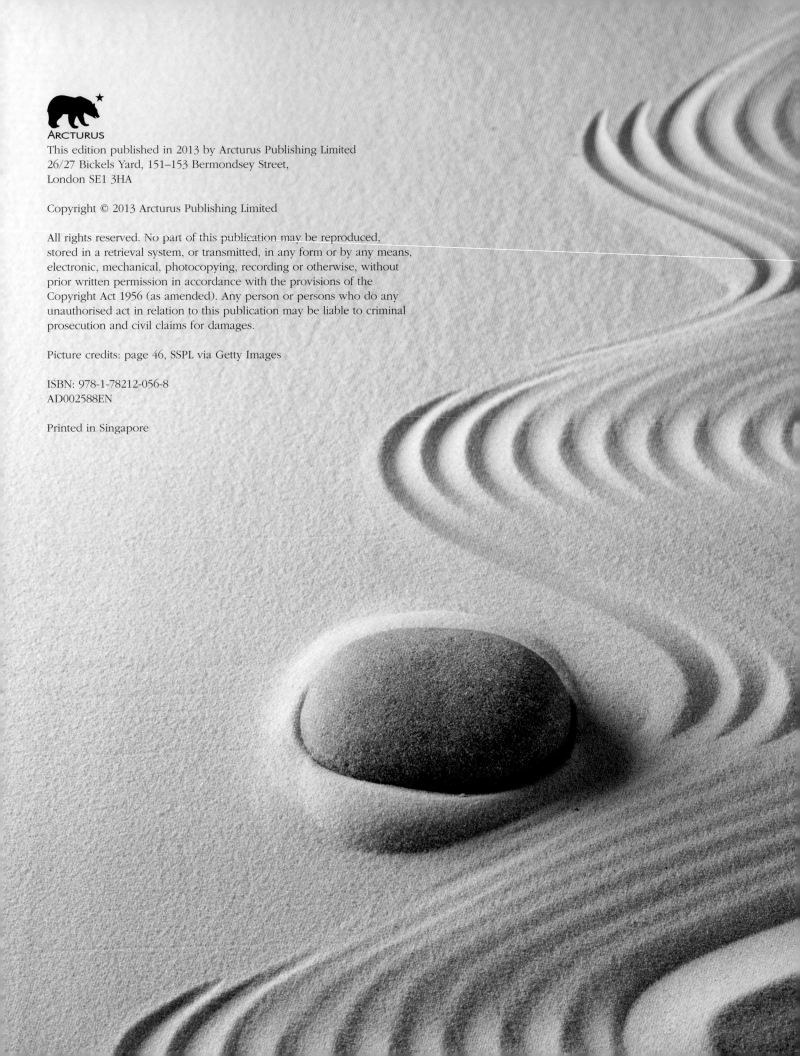

ARCTURUS

This edition published in 2013 by Arcturus Publishing Limited
26/27 Bickels Yard, 151–153 Bermondsey Street,
London SE1 3HA

Picture credits: page 46, SSPL via Getty Images

ISBN: 978-1-78212-056-8
AD002588EN

Printed in Singapore

Contents

CHAPTER ONE

What Are Psychic Powers?

How many times in your life have you said of yourself 'I must be psychic?' When you were thinking of someone and a moment later they phoned you or you bumped into them in the street? When you knew someone was going to say or do something just before they did it? Or perhaps you have had that feeling of 'déjà vu': when something happens that you know has already happened in a dream? The examples are endless and they aren't just coincidences.

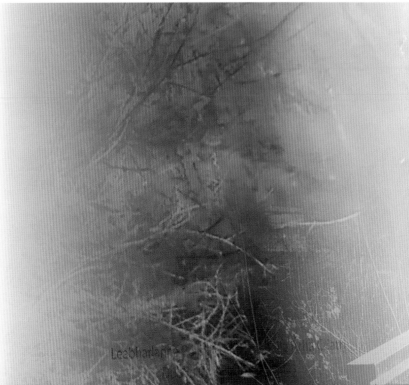

AN INNATE GIFT

The truth is that we all have an inner psychic. It isn't some 'special' or 'supernatural' gift possessed by only a chosen few. Nor should it be confused with witchcraft, magic spells or sorcery. It is within us when we are born and it is our choice whether we explore it or let it lie dormant. So although we often refer to people developing psychic powers, the terminology is slightly misleading because what you are really doing is discovering a part of yourself that is already there, a hidden 'inner' part of you.

Perhaps you have already read something on the subject or discussed psychic phenomena with friends, or maybe you just have a general feeling that there is more out there in the world than meets the eye. Perhaps you feel as though part of you isn't being used, or maybe you're just curious. Hopefully this book will start you thinking about aspects of life you hadn't considered before; it may even set you on the path of psychic awareness which may become a fundamental part of your life.

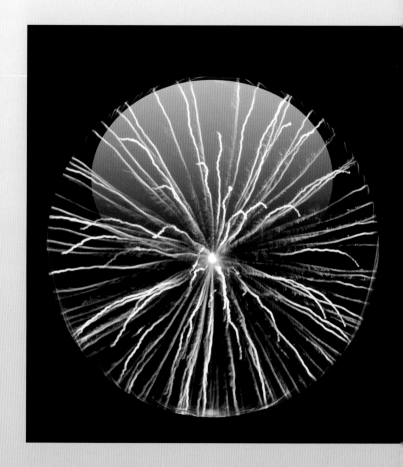

PERSONAL GOALS

It's important to look at what you really want to get out of discovering your inner psychic, because the clearer you are the more it will help your progress. Everyone reading this will be at different stages in their psychic growth; aiming towards your own personal goals will help you to focus.

Let's start by discovering what your inner psychic
can do for you:

1. It's a great form of discipline so it can
   strengthen and focus your mind.
2. It's a 'mind-expanding' experience, which will
   help increase your awareness of the universe.
3. It can be a way to replenish your energy, to
   leave you refreshed and better balanced.
4. It can teach you how to protect yourself
   better on a day-to-day basis and avoid being
   'drained' by influences around you.
5. It will enable you to 'tune in' to other people so
   you can develop a greater understanding
   of them.
6. By enabling you to 'read' other people, it
   means you can learn more about yourself and
   those around you.
7. It can be a form of healing to comfort others.
8. It can be a guide to help solve problems.
9. It can be an unselfish, loving act of giving to
   and helping others.

Certain skills must be developed before psychic work
can be practised safely. When undertaken sensitively
and responsibly, the work can be wonderfully
rewarding and enjoyable. The aim of this book is
to start you off on the psychic path and take you
somewhere you would never have dreamt possible.

It's important to look at what you really want to get out of discovering your inner psychic, because the clearer you are the more it will help your progress.

HOW TO ENJOY THIS BOOK

It is advisable not to rush through the early parts of the book to get to the 'good bit' of actually trying out your psychic energy. Doing so will hamper your progress. Psychic work is a very powerful process and unless you understand some ground rules before you start, it could prove a confusing and even distressing experience. You can liken it to learning to drive: that first moment when you get behind the wheel of a car. All you really want to do is take off and zoom down the road. It's frustrating not to be able to do that, but you know if you try it you're likely to end up in a nasty accident. Plenty of 'psychic accidents' can occur, too, if you don't take 'lessons'. Also, if you only half-complete the exercises, your psychic experiences will be diminished and you'll be disappointed with your results.

To get the maximum benefit from this book, the best thing you can do is to read it first, carefully and in its entirety, without trying any of the exercises. Then reread it and start the exercises. Alternatively, try the exercises in each section as you first read through them, then notice how much more effectively you perform them second time round.

It is also very important that you are drug and alcohol free when trying any of the exercises. This will keep you safe and ensure that your experiences are pleasant.

A WORD OF CAUTION

Now have a look at a few things your inner psychic cannot do for you:

1 Predict the future with certainty (it can only give probability patterns, because each of us has power over his or her own life to change things).
2 Provide a fast answer to all life's problems.
3 Create a good laugh while you fool around with different people and different psychic phenomena.
4 Give you power over other people to make them do what you want them to do.

This last point is particularly important because it's very tempting, once you start discovering your strength, to want to use psychic means to change people around you! But whether it's for your own personal gain or theirs, it won't work.

KARMA AND REINCARNATION

To appreciate why this is so, you need to understand 'karma': cause and effect. The word karma is from the Sanskrit, meaning 'action' (some translate it as 'deed' or 'fate'). Karma can be summed up by the popular expression 'as you sow, so shall you reap'. In other words, everything we think, say and do becomes part of an energy or force that we send out into the universe, and that energy will then return to us. Put simply, if you do harm to others, harm will come to you. If you give out love, then love comes back to you. It's also said that whatever you send out returns to you with doubled intensity.

While karma can rebound in a wonderfully positive way, sometimes you may feel your good actions aren't always reciprocated. You'll no doubt be able to think of many occasions when life isn't at all fair. You now need to go into this more deeply by considering the concept of reincarnation. This is the belief that when our physical body dies our soul lives on and is then reintroduced into other physical bodies. In other words, our soul is separate from our physical being. Our soul is everlasting and constantly in a state of growth and change. We live different physical lives because our soul has many lessons to learn and cannot learn them all in one lifetime. If we

believe our karma travels with us from life to life, it also explains why some people lead troubled lives, without apparent explanation. They are following their own karmic route, influenced by past lives, details of which they probably don't recollect.

If you don't feel that you can believe in the idea of reincarnation it won't stop you from discovering your inner psychic, but it will make your progress slower and there will come a point where you can't progress any further. You will only be able to work at a certain level, that is the emotional level, discussed later in this book. Embracing the concept of reincarnation, together with karma, gives a shape and purpose to our lives. It makes us take responsibility for our own existence and gives us a desire to want to learn, to want to achieve higher levels of consciousness.

A PERSONAL BENEFIT

As you work with your inner psychic, you will appreciate how much of the initial work is about tuning in to others and understanding their emotional, mental and physical states. This is a significant part of your development because so often what we say of others and their current situation can apply to how we lead our own lives. It's believed that we attract to ourselves what we need to learn and grow. So, if you choose to give psychic readings to others, you will find that through them you may learn a great deal about yourself. This doesn't mean you should think of yourself while you are doing the reading, because this would stop your flow of energy which you need for psychic work. But after you've finished, have a little quiet time to yourself to contemplate what you have offered to that other person. How much of it relates to you? How could you make that advice benefit your own life? It's much easier to give advice than to take it. Psychic discovery gives you an opportunity to stop and think on that personal level.

CHAPTER TWO:

Harnessing Energy

In this chapter we are going to discover how you can harness your own energy through awareness of your chakras, and how to draw upon outside energies to guide and replenish you. This interaction of energies is vital for you to develop psychically. There is an exercise to help you connect with each chakra, although it's important to read through the whole chapter first before trying the exercises.

ALONE OR WITH A PARTNER?

At this stage you need to consider whether you want to start your development by working with someone else or on your own. Both alternatives have

advantages. Two or more people can encourage one another and increase confidence levels. One person can volunteer to read and guide the other through the exercises, which can be helpful to begin with. Obviously it's less lonely to share the new experience with someone else. Conversely, if the match isn't right you may inhibit each other. As we all work at different rates and in different ways, this can lead to confusion initially and may make one of you feel less talented than the other. So decide what feels right for you.

If you've made the decision to work with someone, ensure that you both read the book. It isn't a good idea for just one of you to read it and pass on the information because you may unwittingly leave out vital details.

HOW PSYCHIC ENERGIES WORK

The next stage is to learn some basic details. Just as when you start learning to drive you need to know the fundamental parts of the car – ignition, gears, indicators and so on – you also need to know about the fundamental parts of your inner psychic engine. First we are going to look at how we turn our ignition to propel our psychic engine into action; then we will move on to learning how to fill our tanks with psychic 'petrol' so that we can work effectively.

So how do we start our psychic engine? Our key in the ignition takes the form of our mind opening

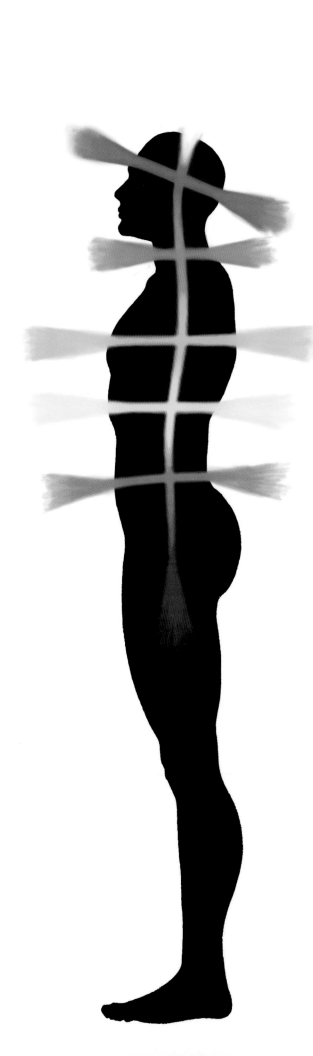

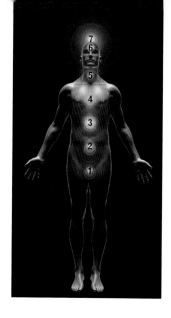

1. Base chakra (Muladhara)
2. Sacral chakra (Swadhisthana)
3. Solar plexus chakra (Manipura)
4. Heart chakra (Anahata)
5. Throat chakra (Vishuddha)
6. Third eye chakra (Ajna)
7. Crown chakra (Sahashara)

up our 'chakras', also known as our energy centres. Unlike a car, which has only one ignition, we have seven major chakras of equal importance and all need to be 'fired' to produce a beneficial flow of energy for psychic work. A highly developed psychic can open all seven throttles within a second, but a beginner takes considerably longer.

Let us delve into these chakras and start our journey to our inner psychic.

CHAKRAS

The seven chakras are interconnecting centres that flow through the body. It helps to think of the chakras as cone-shaped, with streams of energy whirling in through the wide part of the cone and flowing round the body via connecting 'pipes'. Imagine pure, white light and energy whirling in through the cones and filling your body. This is what you will be doing later when you start filling yourself with the psychic petrol we have mentioned. Now look at the illustration (left). Notice how the first chakra (at the base of the spine) opens downwards and the seventh chakra (at the crown of the head) opens upwards and see how they connect through to each other. The other five chakras open front and back horizontally through the body, the second just below the navel, the third through the solar plexus, the fourth through the heart, the fifth through the throat and the sixth through the forehead.

You have to learn how to open these chakras and draw in the psychic petrol to connect with your inner psychic. If this last paragraph and the diagram on the previous page still seem confusing, please study both in detail again before continuing. Don't move on until you feel comfortable with the concept. Now let's look at the chakras in more detail.

The word chakra comes from the Indian Sanskrit, meaning 'wheel'. This is helpful to know because each cone spins like a wheel as we open the energy centre. The chakra is also likened to the lotus, a beautiful flower similar to a lily, with many petals. The lotus as a symbol of the chakras has a deeply spiritual meaning, as this flower can flourish in muddy, dirty waters. It shows us that, however difficult our past, we can move forward to blossom and thrive. Opening a chakra is like opening the petals of a flower, an analogy we use during the upcoming exercises.

There are actions, elements, colours and Sanskrit names connected to each chakra, and each one is linked to part of our anatomy. Now let's look at the chakras individually. Don't worry if what follows seems unclear initially – just keep reading and rereading until you have grasped the salient points.

1. BASE CHAKRA (MULADHARA)

The base chakra is located at the base of the spine and its associated colour is red. It opens downwards to the ground and is always open, but when we tune in to our inner psychic it needs to be opened more, like a fan turning on a low speed that needs to be switched to high. Its Sanksrit name is 'Muladhara' ('mula' means 'root' or 'foundation'), which is very apt as this chakra represents how we relate to the physical world and our sense of belonging within it.

Embedded here is our human determination to have our basic needs met, and our primal survival instinct. The associated element is Earth, and the chakra's physical connection is to the large intestine and excretion, as well as the functions of the legs, feet and bones. The associated action is 'I have'.
The animal often used to symbolize this chakra is the grey elephant, because of its heavy physical mass and solid energy.

EXERCISE – BASE CHAKRA

Make sure you are sitting comfortably in an upright, padded chair, with the soles of your feet firmly on the floor. Take a few deep breaths and settle yourself. Close your eyes and allow yourself to relax into the chair by tuning into the comforting rhythm of your breathing.

Now bring your focus to your base chakra, at the base of your spine. Imagine a cone of energy opening and flowing downwards to the ground. See the vortex of energy spinning and allow it to speed up a little if you wish. Enjoy a sense of being connected to, and grounded by, the Earth's energy below you. Picture a red flower and visualize it at your base chakra. See four petals on that flower slowly unfold and open, allowing the rich colour of red to fill that part of your body. Feel your connection to the Earth's energy strengthen and let it instil in you a sense of belonging.

What do you think of the colour red? What does it mean to you? What do you have around you in your daily life that is red?

Feel your connection to the Earth's energy strengthen and let it instil in you a sense of belonging.

If you think of wearing red clothing, how does that make you feel?

Now consider your relationship with your own physical body. How much do you nurture and appreciate it? When are you most relaxed with your body? Why? Acknowledge all of your physical body and give thanks for its support.

Reflect now on your attitude to nature. How often do you find time to connect with the beauty of what exists naturally around you? When was the last time you watched a sunset or walked by the sea? Or took a walk in a beautiful wood or garden? How do you feel when you connect with nature?

Now visualize a grey elephant. What do you think of when you picture one? How would you describe its energy? Imagine what it might be like to inhabit an elephant's body. Allow yourself to rest in that solid energy for a while.

When you feel ready, you are going to leave the base chakra. To do this, imagine the four petals of your red flower gently folding inwards and closing up; as you do so, the spinning vortex of your base chakra's energy centre gradually slows down without stopping completely. Notice how comfortable and relaxed your body feels and know that you can open up the four petals of your red flower again, whenever you want to meditate on your base chakra. Realize that you will want to return some time, to connect with it further.

If you wish, you can now move on to the sacral chakra exercise. Or, if you want to stop, then focus on how heavy your weight feels in the chair and feel how solid the floor is beneath the soles of your feet. Tune in to your breathing again and become aware of its comforting rhythm. When you're ready, open your eyes and take several minutes to reorientate yourself. Make sure your body feels heavy and comfortable before you stand up.

A LITTLE REASSURANCE

The sacral chakra can make you feel vulnerable or emotional, particularly if intimacy with others is of great importance to you or something you struggle with. If, when you open your eyes after the exercise, you still feel uncomfortable in any way, take time to focus on your breathing and release any emotion with every breath you let out. See the unwanted energy disappear into the distance and make sure you feel grounded and secure before getting up to continue your day.

2. SACRAL CHAKRA (SWADHISTHANA)

The sacral or sacrum chakra is located just below the navel and its associated colour is orange. Its Sanskrit name is 'Swadhisthana', which can be translated as 'sacred home of the self'. This chakra is about how our feelings manifest themselves, particularly in relation to our sexuality and our ability to form and share intimate relationships with others. The associated element is water, so it's perhaps not surprising that this chakra relates to all our bodily fluids and our reproductive systems. The sacral chakra is also called the 'feeling centre', taking in our emotions, and therefore its emotion is said to be 'I feel, I want'. The animal often associated with it is the crocodile, because of its ability to go deep into waters and then resurface.

EXERCISE — SACRAL CHAKRA

As before, take time to settle yourself in your chair and tune in to the comfortable rhythm of your breathing for a minute or two before closing your eyes. Make sure both your feet are flat on the floor.

Focus on the location of your sacral chakra: it is just below your navel. It has two openings, one at the front and one at the back. These cones of energy are usually closed, so we have consciously to open them when we want to spend time with our inner psychic. Before you do this, consider what you feel about your own navel. What is connected to it? Gently touch the area just below your navel. How does that make you feel? Now gently touch the area on your lower back where the back of your sacral chakra opens. How does that feel? If you experience anything uncomfortable, focus on your breathing and imagine the discomfort dissolving away every time you breathe out.

When you are ready, create an image of a beautiful orange flower in your mind's eye. This flower has six petals. Slowly unfold each of the petals and allow the colour orange to flow through your two sacral energy centres. Notice what sensations fill you as you do this and wash away anything you don't want as you breathe out.

Now think about the colour orange. What does it represent to you? How much orange do you have around you? When do you wear the colour orange? What fruits and vegetables do you eat regularly that are orange in colour?

As you allow the colour orange to fill your sacral chakra, both front and back, reflect on your relationships with others. How easy do you find intimacy, sexual or otherwise? How close are your bonds with family and friends? How does being very close to another person, physically and emotionally, make you feel? If any unwanted feelings come to you at this time, remember to wash them away as you breathe out.

What does the image of a crocodile mean to you? What does its energy feel like? Imagine being a crocodile and sinking below the surface of the water for periods of time before resurfacing again. How does that make you feel?

When you think you have spent enough time on this chakra, picture the six petals of your orange flower slowly closing up, one by one. As you do so, visualize the cones of energy, front and back, just below your navel, slowly stopping their spinning action and see them come to a complete stop. Make sure the orange flower petals are tightly closed. If you want to, gently pat both the front and back of your sacral openings with your hand and check they feel closed and secure.

If you wish, move on to the solar plexus chakra exercise or, to stop the exercise, focus on your body and how heavy it feels before you slowly open your eyes.

3. SOLAR PLEXUS CHAKRA (MANIPURA)

The location of the solar plexus (or spleen) chakra is difficult to explain exactly, but it is approximately 13cm (5in) above the navel and 7.5cm (3in) to the left of it. For simplicity, chakras are often depicted drawn in a straight line up the body, but this is not strictly accurate. This chakra opens front and back, but it is not naturally open all the time. Its associated colour is yellow. Used together, the Sanksrit words 'mani' (jewel) and 'pura' (city) translate as 'city of jewels'. The solar plexus energy centre represents our sense of self in relation to our purpose, destiny and willpower. This chakra is connected to our ego and our right to be an individual. Physically it relates to our digestive system, liver, spleen and stomach. This centre is also very much about our emotions in relation to self-will and determination, so it's not surprising that the element here is fire and the action associated with it is 'I can'. The animal often linked with this chakra is the ram, because its energy indicates willpower and determination.

EXERCISE – SOLAR PLEXUS CHAKRA

Make sure you are comfortably settled in your chair, with feet flat on the floor, and connect with the rhythm of your breathing before you continue.

Close your eyes and focus on where you think your solar plexus chakra is located. Run your fingers gently over the area above and to the left of your navel. Where can you feel any sensations? Let your fingers play along the left midsection of your back too. Where do you feel a connection? What do you think of when you reflect on the words 'solar plexus'?

When you feel ready, create a beautiful yellow flower in your mind and notice it has ten petals. Gently open all the petals and, as you do so, feel the warmth of the colour yellow spread through that area of your body. Remember to let the colour radiate through both energy centres, front and back. Observe the cones of energy opening and spinning and enjoy this sensation.

Consider the colour yellow and what it represents to you. How often do you wear clothing or accessories that have yellow in them? Are there any areas where you work or relax that are decorated in yellow? How does that make you feel? What in nature is yellow? How connected do you feel to those yellow elements?

Now think about your position in life and the environment in which you live. How much of it reflects who and what you really are? What does the word 'willpower' represent to you? When you think of your destiny, what images or sensations come to you? If you had to describe your life's purpose, how would you do so? When you set out determined to accomplish a task, how often do you have the energy to complete it? What does the word 'authority' mean to you? Wash away with your out breath anything you would rather not retain.

Consider the energy of a ram and picture one in front of you. Where can you identify with their energy? Where is there a disconnect? What do their horns symbolize to you?

When you are ready, slowly focus on the solar plexus chakra in your body and, one by one, close up the ten petals of your yellow flower. Feel the cones front and back slowly stop spinning and make sure both centres feel closed and secure. Pat your chakra openings gently with your hand, if it feels right to do so, and ensure you feel comfortable.

Now either ground yourself, making sure your body feels heavy in the chair before you get up, or focus on your breathing and continue to the fourth chakra.

4. HEART CHAKRA (ANAHATA)

The heart chakra is located in the middle of the breastbone and its associated colour is green. It opens both front and back through the body. It is not usually open, and we have to open it for psychic work, although strong emotional bursts of receiving and giving love can set these energy cones spinning without our realizing it. While the first three chakras concern our basic needs and emotions, this chakra is where our energy vibration starts to change and becomes a little finer. For example, you could say that chakras 1, 2 and 3 are like heavy, medium-weight and light cotton and chakra 4 is a finer silk. This is not to say that one chakra is better or of more use than another – all have to work together to achieve a harmonious balance. The Sanskrit word here is 'anahata', which translates as 'unstruck sound'. This is particularly apt, as the word implies that life is full of subtle vibrations of sound and we need to tune in to them to live fully. This centre is about compassion and understanding and acts as a sort of hinge between our base levels (our physical body) and our higher, mental levels (our spiritual body). We know that the heart represents love, but in this context the heart chakra isn't just about human love, it's also to do with a larger, universal love that is unconditional and limitless. On a physical level, this centre relates to the circulatory system. Its associated element is air, which is relevant because this energy centre is about openness, lightness and breathing fully to expand our consciousness. The action is 'I love'. The animal often symbolized here is a gazelle, which represents a lightness of energy and a gentle demeanour. It is seen as a creature that can leap over petty behaviour.

EXERCISE — HEART CHAKRA

Sit comfortably in your chair with the soles of your feet firmly on the ground. This time, as you close your eyes, take a little longer to connect with your breath and to focus on its rhythm. The more you concentrate, the deeper and more comfortable your breathing and the better your connection with your heart chakra will be.

Enjoy the sensation of your chest expanding and contracting with each breath. Feel your body relax. Now let your fingers rest on the front opening of your heart chakra, in the middle of your chest. What sensations come to you as you do this? Loving emotions may well up as you focus on the heart chakra. Allow these emotions to manifest, provided they do not distress you. If you feel uncomfortable, focus again on your breath and release anything unwanted each time you breathe out. Place your hand on the back opening of your heart chakra, if you can reach it. If not, simply focus your mind on where it is. Let your breath flow in and out through these two openings and enjoy the feelings of peace and openness that descend as you do so.

Now visualize a beautiful green flower and give it twelve petals. Count through the petals as you open them and feel the colour green wash through your heart chakra, front and back. Focus on the colour green and what it means to you. How often do you have that colour around you? How does it make you feel when you wear green? Reflect on everything in nature that is green. Consider the word 'love'. What does it mean to you? What sensations do you feel as you speak the word? Consider the people in your life whom you love and who love you. Give thanks for their love. Allow your thoughts to expand to consider unconditional love and compassion for others, whatever their behaviour. Now think about appreciating nature and the universe for their wonderful gifts and magical energy. How does your heart chakra feel as you do that? Let yourself rest in this state of appreciation for a while.

Now picture a gazelle in front of you. Observe its gentle energy and lightness of movement. What would it feel like to have that speed? What earthly cares would you have to shed in order to feel so light? Immerse yourself in that lighter energy.

When you are ready, gently remove your focus from your heart chakra by carefully closing the twelve petals. Make sure they all stay closed and that the cones stop spinning front and back. Place your hand over your heart chakra and make sure you feel contained and calm. As the energy with this chakra is lighter and finer and the cones spin faster, you may take longer to ground yourself. Focus firmly on the weight of your body in the chair and the soles of your feet on the floor. Shake your limbs and focus on an object in front of you. Do not stand up again until you are aware of your body and how it feels.

5. THROAT CHAKRA (VISHUDDHA)

The throat chakra is located at the base of the throat, in the little hollow, and its associated colour is sky blue. It opens front and back, but is not normally open. This chakra becomes even finer in vibration than the heart and is demonstrated by the Sanskrit word 'vishuddha', meaning 'pure place'. The throat centre is all about speech, communication, creativity and self-expression. It's not just about our ability to talk, but about how we purify our speech, the care with which we speak and the purpose of our speech. It's to do with listening to our own inner voice and meditation. It's also part of sound and vibrations. The throat centre's physical connection is to the respiratory system and the element associated with it is ether. Expansion is an important part of this chakra: indeed, the limitless expanse of the sky is referenced by its blue colour. Its associated action is 'I speak'. The animal often linked with this chakra is the white elephant. Unlike the solid energetic mass of the grey elephant in the base chakra, this white elephant represents patience, self-confidence and memory. Whereas the grey elephant is usually depicted wearing a collar, indicating its energy being shackled to the earth, the white elephant is collarless, demonstrating freedom from earthly ties that then allow it to embrace its spirituality.

EXERCISE – THROAT CHAKRA

Take time to settle your energy and focus on your breathing before you open your throat chakra. When you feel ready, close your eyes and visualize the energy of this chakra, which is at the base of your throat and opens front and back. Gently touch both openings of the chakra, being careful not to make yourself feel restricted. Swallow. What sensations come over you as you do this? Feel your breath flowing through this energy centre and sense your throat relaxing and opening. As the energy becomes finer here, it may take more practice fully to experience the throat chakra. You may only feel a few sensations at first, but they will increase with time.

Visualize a beautiful blue flower with sixteen petals. Open the petals one by one and, as you do so, place the flower at the hollow of your throat and see the pure colour of sky blue radiating through the chakra, becoming more vibrant with the unfolding of each petal. When all sixteen are fully open, enjoy the sensation of your throat expanding and connecting with the ether around you.

Now concentrate on the colour sky blue. What sensations come over you as you do so? Think about the blue sky and its limitless expanse. What if you lived your life as though it were an endless sky with no boundaries? How does that make you feel? Think about blue oceans, lakes, rivers and streams. Where have you chosen to have blue around you? When do you wear blue?

Consider how you express yourself through speech. How much does what you say reflect who you truly are? How often do you say what other people expect, rather than what you mean? When you feel creative, how does that manifest itself in speech? How often do you consider your words before you articulate them? What power do you believe words have once they are spoken? Reflect upon the opposite: the power of silence. How do you respond to silence? How would you react if you were asked to sit in absolute silence for a period of time?

Now picture a white elephant in front of you. If you had to describe the spiritual essence of an elephant, what qualities would you give it? How do those qualities reflect who you are?

Focus on your sixteen-petalled blue flower and slowly fold up the petals, one by one. Touch your throat chakra, front and back, making sure it feels protected and comfortable. Orientate yourself back in the 'real' world by making sure your body feels heavy and relaxed in your chair. Wriggle your limbs, move your shoulders and rotate your neck gently. Clear your throat and swallow a few times. Stamp your feet. Drink some water when you get up, especially if your throat feels dry.

6. THIRD EYE CHAKRA (AJNA)

The third eye chakra is located in the middle of the forehead and its associated colour is purple or indigo. This chakra opens front and back and needs to be opened consciously when you do psychic work. The third eye chakra is finer again in vibration than the throat centre and its Sanskrit word is 'ajna' which means 'beyond wisdom'. Some call it 'the perception centre', which ties in with references to the third eye or the 'eye of the mind'; this chakra takes us on to yet a greater spiritual realm and higher functions of consciousness connected with intuition, visions and dreams. Because this energy centre is a finer energy, it is not directly related to a physical system within the body the way the other chakras are. Rather it is attuned to the mind, eyes and brain and comes under the heading 'cognition'. Again, we're not talking about the sort of knowing that comes from a material source, but a higher degree of wisdom and vision, attainable only through spiritual development. The element is light and, as meditative processes become all-important here, together with the ability to see our dreams and visions in their deeper spiritual context, so the action is 'I see'. Since this chakra is about non-earthly elements of life, there is no animal associated with it.

EXERCISE – THIRD EYE CHAKRA

With the third eye chakra, the energy again becomes finer and lighter so you need to focus even more. Ensure you are not interrupted. Allow a minimum of fifteen minutes for this exercise so that you can reflect deeply and ground and reorientate yourself afterwards. Begin by focusing on the centre of your forehead. Keeping your eyes closed, imagine that there is a third eye in the middle of your brow. Breathing deeply and comfortably, look through your third eye. What do you see? Wash away anything you don't want as you breathe out; see it dissolve into nothingness. Gently touch the middle of your forehead and hold your fingers there for a moment. What sensations do you have? Now place your fingers on the third eye chakra opening at the back of your head and notice what you sense/see as result.

Keeping your breathing deep and slow, create a beautiful, vivid purple flower with two large petals. These petals symbolize a pair of wings, through which your mind can release itself from earthly bonds and fly into spiritual realms, transcending time and space. As you carefully unfold each petal or wing, allow the rich spiritual essence of the colour purple to flow through your third eye. Observe the effect of this colour on your mind and body. How does it make you feel?

Now your wings are fully extended you are free to allow higher consciousness to flow through your third eye chakra. Slowly fill yourself with the colour purple. Imagine it filling your body with light and wisdom. Notice any signs, symbols or messages that float through your third eye chakra. Don't try to interpret them, just give thanks for their presence and observe how they make you feel. Allow yourself to receive without consciously straining to find anything. Keep breathing deeply and calmly. Let yourself sit in this peaceful state for as long as you can.

When you are ready, carefully bring your thoughts to focus on the purple flower and its two large petals. Slowly and deliberately fold one petal and then the other. Make sure they stay closed. Feel the colour purple receding from every part of your body and being replaced by a pure white energy. Focus on both cones of energy and make sure they have stopped spinning and are closed like your flower.

When you feel empty and relaxed, focus on the weight of your buttocks on your chair and the soles of your feet on the floor. You may feel a slight 'thump' in your body as you become grounded. If, when you open your eyes, you feel light-headed, press your feet firmly on the floor and feel the blood flowing through your legs. Focus on an object in the room and make sure your eyes register it clearly. Don't get up straight away. Pat yourself all over, particularly down your arms and legs. When you get up, make sure your feet feel solid on the ground before you walk. Drink a glass of water.

GROUNDING YOURSELF WITH 'ROOTS'

As you move up through the chakras, because the energy becomes brighter and finer, you may find it more difficult to ground yourself after you have tuned in. This is normal, but it is important to take the time to reorientate yourself afterwards. Getting up quickly could result in you feeling dizzy, which would be unnerving. Make sure your body feels heavy and your feet feel anchored to the ground before you stand. A good tip is to imagine that you have roots growing out of the soles of your feet and that they are embedded deep into the Earth's surface, making you feel solid and secure and very 'earthbound'. You also might find it helpful to imagine a pink light coming up from deep within the Earth's core and connecting your feet firmly to Earth's gravity. Provided you take time to do this, you can feel confident about continuing your exploration of your inner psychic.

7. CROWN CHAKRA (SAHASHARA)

The seventh chakra is situated just above the crown of your head. It has the highest, finest energy of all the chakras. Its associated colour is white, but it is sometimes depicted as violet. It has one opening, upwards to the sky, and it remains open at all times, although we need to speed up its vibration in order to work psychically. It is through this chakra that we fill ourselves with the 'psychic petrol' mentioned earlier in this section. The Sanskrit word 'sahashara' means 'thousandfold' or 'infinite', so it is apt that this chakra flower has a thousand petals. The crown chakra is about self-realization and fulfilment; it also represents completion, as it is the highest state and can only function in the fullest sense with an open mind, using truth and sincerity. This is the hardest chakra to describe in words as it can only really be experienced. It is also the only chakra that is not within our physical body, further demonstrating that it does not relate to earthly matters but reflects a state known as 'bliss'. This is achieved through prolonged spiritual growth and is outside the comprehension of most of us who do not meditate. For now it's enough to consider it a concept towards which we can strive! The element associated with the crown chakra is thought and its action is 'I know'. There is no physical part of the body, nor any animal, connected to this energy centre because it transcends physical boundaries and vibrates at the highest frequency.

The crown chakra is about self-realization and fulfilment; it also represents completion.

EXERCISE — CROWN CHAKRA

As this is the highest and finest vibrational energy centre, you need to be in the right frame of mind to focus on the crown chakra. You might want to do this on a separate day so that you can focus fully or just wait until the time feels right. As with all the chakra exercises, you need to find the time to sit quietly first. Let your body settle gently into your upright chair, making sure you shake or wriggle any tension from your limbs first. Plant both feet firmly on the ground and make sure they stay there throughout. Close your eyes and focus on your breathing. Make an extra effort to let go of any worries or concerns you have, knowing you can have them back when you finish! Enjoy feeling relaxed and comfortable. Take your time.

When the time feels right, bring your focus to the space about 7.5cm (3in) above the crown of your head. As this is your first experience of focusing on an area outside your physical body, don't worry if you feel very little at first. Keep breathing and concentrate on that area. Visualize a cone above your head opening upwards to the sky and see the cone opening wider and spinning more quickly, until it whirrs on a high speed.

Create your beautiful white flower with thousands of petals and visualize all those petals opening simultaneously in the cone, releasing a stream of white light that reaches up into the sky and beyond into the universe.

As you do this, realize that the base of the cone has an opening that allows energy to filter down from above. You become aware that your white energy has met with a fine, bright, white energy from deep in the universe and now both white energies are fusing together and pouring down through the opening at the bottom of your crown chakra centre.

Allow this celestial white light to come down into the top of your head through the crown chakra and then, slowly, feel it spreading through to all your chakra centres. Let it radiate down through your head, filling your third eye chakra, front and back. Feel it move down your neck, spreading through your throat chakra, front and back. Enjoy the sensation as it makes its way down your torso, sweeping through your heart, solar plexus, sacral and base chakras, filling your whole body with pure white light.

Whatever inspirational messages or images are given to you during this process, receive them with thanks. Don't linger on them or try to analyse them; allow them to float through and around you and accept these gifts on whatever level you are meant to have them.

Recognize that the white light is spreading down through your arms and your legs. As it reaches the soles of your feet, become aware that this white light is now meeting a pink energy that you are pulling up through the soles of your feet from deep within the Earth's core. Slowly allow this rich pink energy to come up through your legs and spread through your body. Realize these two pink and white energy sources are connecting and fusing together.

Allow these energies to mix and appreciate how you now feel, both anchored by the pink Earth energy and energetically uplifted by the Universal white light, so you feel both grounded and ready for spiritual enlightenment. Sit in this state for as long as you can. Let the grounding and spiritual energies settle where they are most needed and enjoy their gifts.

When the time is right, return your attention to your crown chakra and your beautiful white flower with thousands of petals. Make all the petals close firmly and, when they do, observe how your crown chakra cone slows from its fast whirring speed to a more gentle revolution. When it feels a comfortable speed, slowly go through the rest of your chakras, closing them one by one. If you can't remember the colours initially, then gently pat the chakra areas and imagine them closed and secure. Remember they all need to be closed, apart from the crown and base chakras, which should be slightly open and whirring slowly.

When you feel safely closed down, spend time grounding yourself. Picture strong roots growing out of the soles of your feet and know these roots burrow deep into the earth, making you feel firmly connected to our planet. Use the pink Earth energy to anchor you further if needed. Wriggle all of your body and notice you feel very heavy and comfortable in your chair. Wait a few minutes before you get up and make sure you drink a full glass of water immediately afterwards.

How did you feel after opening your crown chakra? It can be a very heady experience, so it's important to feel properly closed down as you continue with the rest of your day. If you suddenly feel light-headed at any point, focus on the roots growing from the soles of your feet or stamp your feet firmly for a few seconds. You need to ensure you are properly grounded as you go about your daily tasks; you can always return to that uplifting energy again in the future!

You will probably also realize that the 'psychic petrol' mentioned earlier is, in fact, the pure white light you were pulling down through your chakras in the crown chakra exercise! We call this the Universal energy. So now you know how you can fill your psychic engine with petrol.

Much has been written about the source of this Universal energy. For some people, Universal energy has a religious or spiritual significance that strengthens their connection with it. But you don't need to follow a particular belief system to work with your inner psychic. The more you concentrate on connecting with Universal energy, the more powerful it becomes, irrespective of your beliefs.

So these are the seven major chakras, or energy centres, which we need to open in order to draw in the pure, white Universal energy that we can then use to explore our inner psychic. The pink Earth energy that you experienced coming up through the soles of your feet during your crown chakra exercise is what you need to ground you.

THE TWO LEVELS OF PSYCHIC WORK

If you eventually decide to give psychic readings for other people, it is useful to know that psychic work can be divided into two categories. The first, the emotional, relates to the first three chakras, the base, sacral and solar plexus, and in part to the fourth, the heart chakra, which has already been described as a 'hinge' between the base and higher levels. This emotional level of psychic work allows us to develop skills such as psychometry, auric reading and flower reading. The second, higher level is called the mental sphere and involves use of the finer vibrational frequencies of the throat, third eye and crown chakras together, again, with the heart centre. Work on this level is purely with 'spirit', via clairvoyance, clairaudience, inspirational speaking and trance work. We won't be studying this level here, as it would be the equivalent of passing a driving test then immediately hopping behind the wheel of a double-decker bus or a ten-ton lorry and trying to weave through heavy traffic!

Although we are not actively using the throat, third eye and crown chakras in our emotional psychic work, it doesn't mean we leave these energy centres closed. All chakras need to be opened to allow the proper flow of energy through the body.

A CHAKRA SUMMARY

To sum up what we have learned so far – there are seven major chakras in the body that we need to open when we tune in to our inner psychic. We draw pure, Universal energy into our bodies through our crown chakra and work with that energy to develop our psychic abilities. We use the pink Earth energy from deep in the Earth's core to keep us grounded while we work. At the very least, you need to memorize the points below (although the more you can remember from earlier in this section the better):

1 Base. Red. Base of spine. Opens downwards to the earth.
2 Sacral. Orange. Just below the navel. Opens front and back.
3 Solar plexus. Yellow. Above and slightly left of navel. Opens front and back.
4 Heart. Green. Centre of breastbone, above chest. Opens front and back.
5 Throat. Blue. Hollow of throat. Opens front and back.
6 Third eye. Purple. Middle of forehead. Opens front and back.
7 Crown. White or violet. Top of head. Opens upwards to the sky.

For some people, Universal energy has a religious or spiritual significance that strengthens their connection with it. But you don't need to follow a particular belief system to work with your inner psychic.

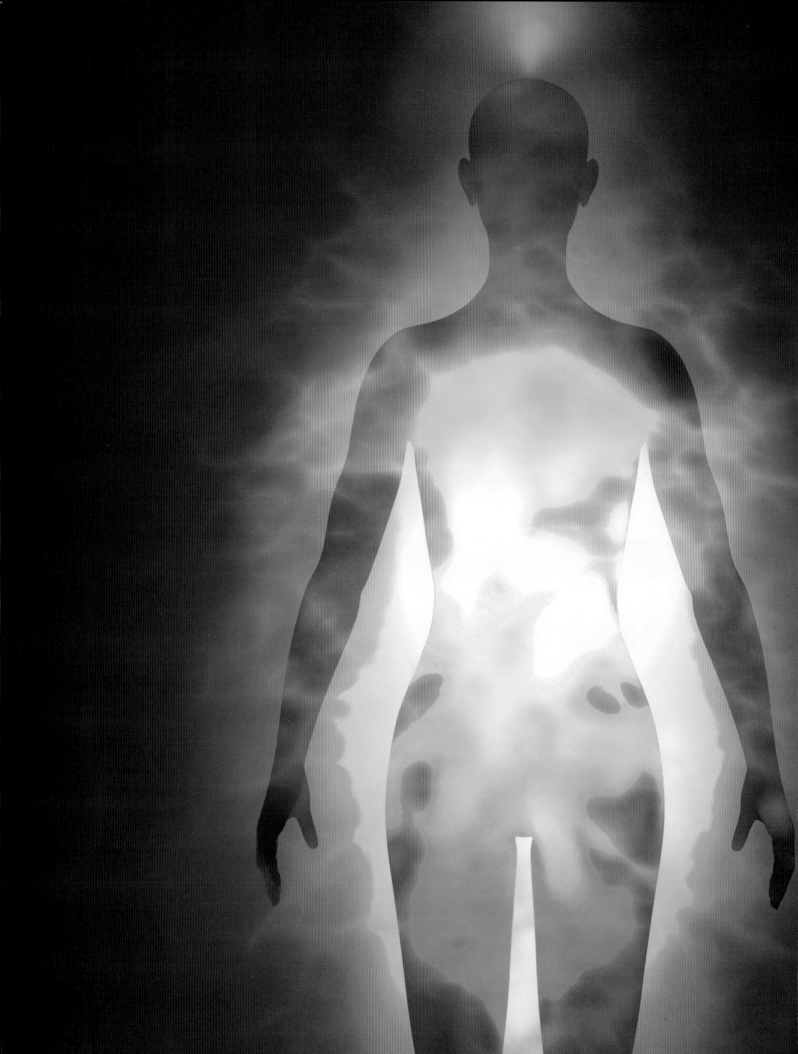

CHAPTER THREE:

Invisible Energies

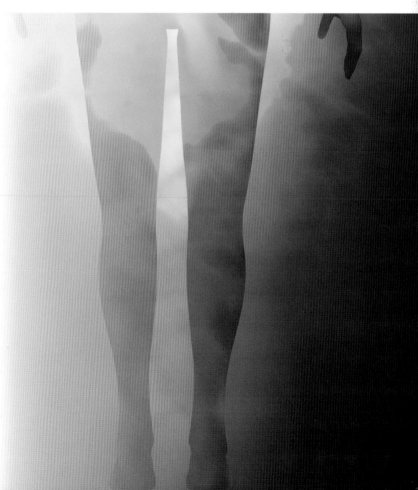

Before we start our exercises to 'open up' and practise psychic work, there's another subject we need to cover: invisible energies. Have you noticed that when someone is head-over-heels in love they seem to exude a warmth, a joy that far exceeds their physical body? It is this kind of unseen energy that we are going to explore in this chapter.

THE AURA

Sometimes called the human energy field, the aura is a layer of energy surrounding the body. It's not normally visible to the layperson but it can be seen once we spend more time with our inner psychic. You have probably been aware of people's auras at some time or other, even though you may not have actually seen one yet. Have you ever felt a change in the atmosphere when someone comes and sits next to you on a train or walks into the room? This is an example of you reacting to someone's aura. Every living object has an aura (as do inanimate objects, but we'll come to that later). Auras are constantly changing – expanding and contracting, and fluctuating with our emotional, mental, spiritual and physical states.

EXERCISE — EXPERIENCING YOUR AURA

Open your palms and fingers flat and place them about 35cm (12in) apart, palm facing palm. Now slowly move your hands towards each other; the longer you take to do this, the more likely you are to enjoy this exercise. Try to breathe rhythmically and deeply as you do so. Don't worry if it takes a few attempts before you feel anything, because the more relaxed you are, the easier it will be to get a response. At some point, before your palms touch, you should feel something – a tingle, a pressure, a warmth, a butterfly-like tickly feeling, or possibly a stronger sensation of force – it will be different for everyone. However it manifests itself to you, this is your own energy fields touching. Now practise moving your hands slowly back and forth, 'playing' with that ball of energy. When does the feeling weaken or disappear? Does it get stronger the more you experiment with it? You can also practise this exercise finger to finger. Afterwards draw circles with your index finger in the palm of the other hand, without touching the skin. Does it tickle?

> There are at least seven levels or bands to the aura, radiating out sequentially from the body and each relating to a different chakra.

HOW AURAS RELATE TO THE CHAKRAS

Our aura is highly intricate and, although we can't study it in detail here, it's important to know that there are at least seven levels or bands to the aura, radiating out sequentially from the body and each relating to a different chakra. The first layer relates to the base chakra, the second to the sacral and so on. Do you remember the chakra cones we talked about in Chapter Two? There isn't just one cone front and back; each layer of the aura has its own pair of cones. They all nestle into one another, like a stack of empty ice-cream cones, through the seven layers. Because of the aura's complexity, some teachers simplify it into three basic sections. Only a highly developed psychic is ever likely to see the aura in its entirety and to study this is a lifetime's work. A novice will probably only see the first level, known as the etheric field, and this is the band which immediately surrounds us, extending 5cm (2in) or so from our physical body. Because this level is the densest (in other words, on the least fine vibration), it's possible during the early stages for you to see it as a hazy vapour around the body.

You may be confused about expressions used in this book such as 'finer vibration' and 'higher frequency', so here's an example to help. Remember how we made reference earlier to a fan whirring on different speeds? Imagine you are looking at an electric fan that is switched off. You can see its propeller blades quite easily. Now imagine it is switched on at a very low speed or low vibrational frequency. You can still see the blades, but they are becoming blurred as they move. Then switch it to a higher speed – they become even more blurred. Turn it to full speed so that you can't distinguish the blades any more. This is how our own energies work in our aura. The faster they whirl, the less we can see: that is, until we become more attuned.

Other 'living' objects such as vegetables, fruit, plants, flowers and trees have auras too.

EXERCISE — SEEING THE AURA OF A LIVING THING

Take any living object (a household plant may be the easiest to begin with), place it against a plain, dark background and shine a light on to it. As you did with the palm exercise, try to breathe slowly and regularly and focus your eyes on the object itself. Try not to stare intently, but let your gaze soften as much as possible, rather as if you were trying to see a 3D picture. After a while you may start to see a hazy glow, or cloud, around the edges of the object. It will probably appear colourless to you but have a luminous quality, as though you were staring into a candle's flame. This is the object's energy. Don't worry if you can't see anything initially. You may need to be tuned in through the exercises before you can open up to this phenomenon.

INANIMATE OBJECTS

It gets even more interesting when you realize that even inanimate objects have an aura too! Their energy comes from vibrational imprints that are placed onto and into them by living objects with which they come into contact. This is important to understand when we come to the section on psychometry. Obviously the energy of inanimate objects is finer and can be infinitely more confusing, because one object may have been handled by many different people. Think of the aura of a coin that has been touched by countless hands!

Fascinating inroads have been made into the study of the aura, particularly in recent years. For example, Kirlian photography is a means of photographing energy fields, usually around the hands. An image is developed and can be used as a diagnostic tool to help someone learn more about themselves. You can also have the aura of your head photographed in colour – if you attend a psychic or spiritual exhibition, you will possibly see this being offered.

BECOMING AWARE OF YOUR AURA

For now, you need to start becoming aware of your own aura. Our aura constantly fluctuates

EXERCISE — EXPANDING YOUR AURA

Sit or stand on your own in a room. Make sure you won't be disturbed by anyone for a few minutes. Now close your eyes and breathe comfortably. Let your thoughts settle and your body relax. Focus on each in breath and out breath, tuning in to its rhythm. At the same time, concentrate on your aura and try to work out where its edges are. A few centimetres from your body? A few metres? Try to pinpoint where it ends. After a few moments, every time you breathe in, imagine your aura expanding outwards, and every time you breathe out imagine it settling comfortably in its newly widened space. Repeat this process for as many breaths as you like and see how much you can expand your aura. Can you make it reach the walls of the room? The ceiling? How do you feel as your aura expands? When you have had enough, reverse the process. Every time you breathe in, feel your aura contracting towards your body. Every time you breathe out, feel it settle closer to you. When your aura feels nicely enclosed around your physical body again, stop. Ground yourself firmly before you open your eyes.

according to our moods and environment; as you start developing your psychic abilities, your aura will expand. You therefore need to learn how to contract it again and protect yourself. If you don't, you can leave yourself very vulnerable to other people's unwanted influences.

So practise becoming aware of your own aura. Do you hate getting into crowded trains or lifts? No wonder, with all those auras squashed together! Notice how, even if a person you like steps too close to you, you feel like taking a few steps away. They've intruded into your aura and it makes you feel uncomfortable. Have you noticed how different spaces have different auras? One room in a house

has a completely different feel from another, especially different bedrooms. Different situations make our auras expand and contract. Can you think of examples when this would happen? Try to notice on a day-to-day basis when you feel your aura has grown or shrunk and consider why this has happened.

As you develop your inner psychic, you will need to expand and contract your aura on a regular basis. To help with this, practise the 'expanding your aura' exercise whenever you have time. Make sure you practise only when no one else around.

When you are ready, you can progress to the exercise on the next page.

EXERCISE — FEELING ANOTHER PERSON'S AURA

If you have chosen to work with a partner, or if you have a willing friend or relative, you can practise feeling another person's aura. Ask your volunteer to stand comfortably in the middle of a room, away from furniture and walls, with their hands loosely by their sides. Ask them to keep their eyes open throughout the experiment, as they might feel dizzy or off-balance otherwise. Now you are going to practise feeling their aura. Remember to breathe regularly and deeply before you start.

When you feel relaxed, start moving your hands around your sitter, a metre or so away from their body. Aim your hands at their solar plexus area, not at their heart or around their head. Do keep your distance to begin with, and then gradually, very gradually, move your hands further in towards them. At what point do you naturally want to stop? Some people's aura will extend over a metre from their body, others less. If you are relaxed and breathing properly, you should feel a somewhat marshmallow-like texture where their aura begins and you should naturally want to stop and not penetrate their aura further. (This is also a useful exercise to increase your feelings of sensitivity and respect towards your sitter). Once you can feel something, move your hands over the rest of their aura. When does it get hotter – or colder – suddenly? Do you feel a sudden pull towards a certain area and sense that you should keep away from other areas? Remember not to spend any time near the heart chakra or over the crown of the head; just pass over those areas lightly.

Once you have explored their aura, ask your volunteer what it felt like for them. Did they have feelings of hot or cold or any uncomfortable or comforting sensations? The more you practise this exercise, preferably with more than one volunteer, the more you will become attuned to auras and appreciate how they are all so different.

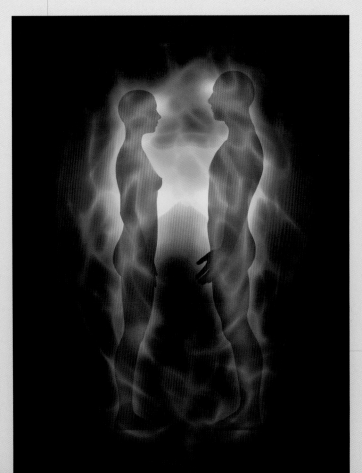

You cannot make your aura disappear completely. It is a mostly invisible, loyal friend that accompanies you everywhere, constantly changing as you change.

RENEW YOUR ENERGIES

In psychic work, you use energies from your own aura to activate your chakras, but you also must draw in the pure white light – the Universal energy – as well. As you 'give out' through your psychic work so you must repeatedly renew your energies. This constant flow of energy is essential for psychic development and for your own wellbeing. Often, inexperienced healers and psychics make the mistake of using only their own energies to help others. They soon end up exhausted and, in some cases, extremely ill.

Remember, also, to balance your energies by using the grounding pink Earth energy to keep you focused and centred. This is what makes your physical body able to work effectively with higher frequencies. This is especially important for beginners in psychic work because once you start tuning in and drawing in the Universal energy it can be a very heady experience! It's a great way to 'fly away with the fairies', but while it can be very pleasant it won't help you in psychic development unless you also have the Earth's energy to keep you solid and focused. So do remember to keep your feet anchored to the ground by visualizing roots growing from the soles of your feet into the earth and drawing up the pink Earth energy, especially if you ever feel a little light-headed. Exercises later on in this book will show in more detail how to cleanse, ground and protect yourself.

You cannot make your aura disappear completely. It is a mostly invisible, loyal friend that accompanies you everywhere, constantly changing as you change.

CHAPTER FOUR:

Creating Your Own Space

Now that you have started to experience the amazing energies inside and around you, your next task is to create the best environment in which to continue your discoveries. If, in time, you want to progress and give readings to others, what we discuss here will be particularly useful. It isn't necessary to follow through on every suggestion in these pages, but the more positive energy you create the quicker your psychic development will be. And making a harmonious environment can improve all aspects of your life, not just the time you spend working on your inner psychic!

TIME

Creating your own space doesn't just mean making a physical area for your work; it's also about creating enough time and emotional space for you to work comfortably. Time is an important issue in psychic development because we are all used to working within the physical timescales we have set up on Earth, so we constantly think about managing the time we use. Our need to box everything into neat time frames means we often forget how to experience time spontaneously. We are so busy thinking about what has happened, or planning and worrying about what is going to happen, that we forget to live in the 'now' of life. So let's start by looking at how you spend your time each day.

After completing the exercise opposite, are you surprised to discover that you seldom take any time for yourself? Many people don't devote time to themselves because it makes them feel guilty. They associate time spent alone with being selfish. Many of us think we are better people if we spend all our time rushing around managing other individuals. Another reason is fear. We aren't sure what we may discover if we stop living our hectic lives and start to spend time thinking. We have areas of our lives that we don't want to look at because, if we did, it might mean we would have to make a change. We tell

ourselves it's better to settle for what we've got. But if this is truly how you feel, you wouldn't be reading this book. You obviously know there is more going on out there and you are prepared for some of the changes that may happen along your path.

EXERCISE — TIME AWARENESS

Take a pen and paper and draw a large circle. This circle represents your day. How do you allocate your time each day? Divide the circle into individual 'pie slices'. Obviously, some days are different from others, but take an average day and work out where you devote your energies. Be honest with yourself; if you spend twelve hours at work, write that down. If you watch television for three or four hours every evening, write that down, too. The more detailed you are, the more you'll be able to see exactly how you use your time. Instead of just dividing the twenty-four-hour period into sleep, work, travel and socializing, specifically itemize your activities. For example:

- How long do you spend getting ready in the morning?
- How much time do you spend eating?
- When do you fit any physical exercise into your day?
- How much time do you spend with family and friends?
- When do you find time for appreciation of nature?
- When do you find time to listen to music?
- How many hours a day do you devote to hobbies?
- How much of your day is spent with other people?
- How much time do you take for quiet reflection?

By the time you get to the last point, your piece of paper will probably be a complete jumble and you'll be wondering how you fit everything into each day.

PHYSICAL CHANGE

One of the changes you need to make is a physical change. You need to find at least fifteen minutes each day that you can call your own, without interruption from outside forces. It should ideally be the same time every day, too. This is an important discipline for you; you have to train your mind to respond to new needs, as well as new ideas. You'll probably encounter a fair amount of resistance along the way. You're probably resisting even as you're reading this, wondering how you can manage even fifteen minutes.

Look at the circle you have drawn on the paper. What isn't necessary in your day? Is there anything that perhaps hinders rather than helps your personal development, which you could reduce or cut out without harming anyone else? Could you get up fifteen minutes earlier each day or go to bed fifteen minutes later, without causing much hardship?

If you keep looking and considering new possibilities you will see how you can find an extra fifteen minutes a day. Try to make it the same time each day and avoid late evenings as you might make your mind too active for sleep afterwards.

ACCEPT YOUR OWN RATE OF PROGRESS

Once you have found your fifteen minutes of free time, you need to be committed to it. Sometimes, during your work on your inner psychic, you might feel discouraged and irritated. Your progress will seem slow and may even seem to go backwards. Don't set yourself goals about your speed of development. Apart from a commitment to fifteen minutes or half-an-hour each day, you won't be able to determine what you will accomplish within any period. You will move forward when the time is right and you have to trust that this is as it should be. Enjoy your own progression, whatever the speed.

Now you have created your quiet time, you need to consider further aspects of yourself that will make your journey to your inner psychic easier. Some of the points made in the following pages may seem obvious but, if you're honest, you probably don't always observe them. Try to incorporate them as much as you can, but be aware that you are also human and imperfect. Do your best, but be kind to yourself when you slip up.

PHYSICAL EXERCISE

First, think about how you look after yourself physically. It is known that physical exercise, taken three times a week, is beneficial. It doesn't have to be the gym or jogging. Take a brisk walk, join a yoga or tai chi class, or maybe take up salsa dancing! Perhaps you feel you haven't spent enough time with someone recently? Take some exercise together and enjoy two positive experiences at once.

SLEEP

At the other end of the spectrum is the need for sleep. This is a personal affair, as we are all different. Some of us need at least eight to ten hours; others operate well on six. Many people can catnap for ten or fifteen minutes and wake up refreshed; others find that if they try to catnap they resurface feeling disorientated and grumpy. Start listening to the needs of your body and learn what works best for you. If you tune in to your own requirements, you really will feel the benefits. You'll have far more energy; every part of you will reap the rewards.

DIET

Now consider what you eat. Different energy foods help you in different ways. How the food is grown is important. We all know that fruit and vegetables are good for us; however, acid rain, pesticides and environmental pollution can diminish much of food's natural energy. If you consume organic produce, you are giving yourself the best chance of high-energy food. Keeping food for too long will also work against you; the auric levels of food drop considerably when it is no longer fresh. Also, overcooking and boiling will burn off energy; steamed vegetables will benefit you far more. As you increase your inner psychic, you will learn to listen to your body more. What food gives you energy? Which foods leave you feeling sluggish afterwards?

Too much of any food will unbalance your energy; and did you know that excessive consumption of stimulants such as alcohol, tea, coffee and fizzy drinks is visible in your aura?

Water is particularly important to our needs – we often overlook its power. Humans are made up of seventy per cent water, the brain is more than ninety per cent water and even our bones are sixty per cent water. Drink as much water and herbal tea as you want throughout the day.

When you work psychically there are a few dietary 'musts'. As mentioned earlier, alcohol and drugs never, ever mix with psychic work. Also try to avoid overeating or being hungry before working with your inner psychic. The more comfortable you are physically, the more effective you will be.

PERSONAL HYGIENE

How particular are you about personal hygiene? This is another area that affects our spiritual and psychic growth. Our skin is the means through which energy flows in and out of our bodies. We need to keep it cleansed and unclogged, preferably using natural, non-toxic products. Oral hygiene and clean hands and nails are also very important, particularly when giving readings. As our physical body is the means through which our spiritual energy flows, our inner psychic works best when we keep ourselves clean and healthy.

CLOTHING

What sort of clothes do you wear? Are they made from natural fibres such as cotton, silk and wool, or are they synthetic? It helps if you choose mostly natural fibres to wear next to your skin – cotton pants, vest and socks, for example. When you are practising psychic work, try to wear loose, comfortable clothing without footwear, apart from socks or tights. For your grounding techniques, you need the soles of your feet to maintain direct contact with the floor.

COLOURS

What colours do you wear? Generally speaking, constantly wearing dark colours tends to deplete your energy field. It makes it harder for you to release unwanted energy and for other energies to penetrate you. To find out what colours are right for you, simply open your wardrobe and look at your clothes. Which do you feel drawn to? After you have done this daily for a week you will probably know what colours you need for nurturing and renewing your energies.

It can help to relate colours to the chakras. Are you planning a sexy evening with your lover and wanting to enhance the energies? Try orange. If you feel your day requires inner strength and a sense of calm, try using some blue. When would purple seem appropriate as a choice? When might you use red?

JEWELLERY

Jewellery is another influencing factor. How often do you put on a piece of jewellery without considering whether its energy is compatible with your own energy fields? Now you understand how every object carries its own energies, this becomes increasingly important. You can check for yourself whether a piece of jewellery is right for you. All you have to do is hold it in the palm of your hand and see what you feel. Is it warm or cold? Does its energy feel sharp and brittle or strong and comforting? Unless the item feels right for you, don't wear it. Hold it against the area where the piece of jewellery will be resting to see if it feels right. If need be, you can cleanse an object of its energies; details of how to do this can be found on page 127.

YOUR PERSONAL SPACE

You need to think about creating a space of your own in which to practise psychic development. The reason this is so important is because your growth is helped enormously by the environment in which you

A jumbled space results in a jumbled mind. An object should be there only if it has a use and is an energy balancer.

are working. By always being in one space, you will constantly be filling that area with your own psychic energy and that will positively impact on you every time you walk into it. It becomes your own haven of safety and comfort, where enlightenment can reach down and touch you easily because you are always 'in tune' while you are there. If there isn't a whole room available to you, try sectioning off part of a room by using a tall screen or bookshelves. Once you have found an area you can call your own, you need to start furnishing it in the way that feels right for you. This is a personal matter, but here are some ideas for you to consider.

Just as colours are important in the clothing you choose, they are also important in creating your own space. If you have the opportunity to colour the walls as you want, then do so. Don't rush the process. If you feel uncertain, buy a small sampler first and test it on a patch of wall. Keep the colour or wallpaper design simple; let your choice enhance your vibrations without confusing them.

If redecorating your space is not a viable option, then try putting up some pictures. Artwork is a powerful form of energy. Again, it's very personal. What resonates well with one person will completely unbalance another. Move some pictures into your private space and see what they feel like there. Has the energy now changed in your room? When you have time, visit art galleries and start looking more closely at paintings. Spiritual awareness also affects art appreciation. You'll be amazed at how much more a painting will mean to you once you have tuned in to its energies.

What furniture and objects do you wish to have within your personal space? You need an upright chair with a padded seat for many of your exercises.

You may want to lie down for others. You may want to have some crystals around you (they're discussed in more detail on page 127) or a sound system for playing music. You may want candlelight. Would you like some plants around you to increase the energy?

A word of warning: a jumbled space results in a jumbled mind. An object should be there only if it has a use and is an energy balancer.

The position of an object in a room is as important as whether it's there at all. Keep going through your space, rearranging and clearing away what you know you don't want. This alone has an amazing effect on the energy in the room. You know how much better you feel after a good clear out, whether it's the contents of your fridge or a whole attic? This isn't just because you have done something you've been meaning to do for ages; it's also because old, stagnant vibrations have been cleared to allow energy to move more freely around and through everything.

LIGHT

Light, both natural and artificial, is another consideration. Sunlight is a powerful energy restorer and balancer. If possible, access natural light within your own space. If it has to be artificial, make the lighting soft. Choose pastel-coloured lampshades and pearl bulbs. The soothing qualities of candlelight are also beneficial, provided you put candles in secure holders.

SOUND

Another good energy balancer is sound. Sound has been used for centuries as a way of focusing the mind and for healing. Many religious groups use chanting as a way to increase awareness; medicine healers of all cultures and countries have used it to balance unwell individuals. You will need to experiment with the wide range of music available to discover what sounds soothe, uplift and inspire you.

Different types of music have been shown to work well with different chakras. For example, drumbeats are said to activate the base chakra, connecting us to our earthly roots. Pop and rock music are said to awaken our sexuality within our sacral chakra. Love songs awaken our heart chakra and harp music is said to benefit the higher chakras.

Experiment to find out what works best for you.

Research has also been done into how sounds are directly related to nature. This is called cymatics. The late Dr Hans Jening conducted a series of experiments whereby he placed fine grains of sand on a metal plate. He then sent a steady, unbroken stream of sound through the plate. The sand formed a distinct pattern. When he changed the sound frequency, the pattern changed. When he returned to the first sound, the sand re-formed into its first pattern. He found this to be a consistent phenomenon – every sound frequency had its own pattern of sand. When the sound was stopped completely, the grains of sand returned to settle according to Earth's gravitational pull.

If you are particularly susceptible to sounds and

find that they help you to focus, then you might like to know that the chakras are associated with the seven notes of the musical scale. The base chakra is said to connect with middle C, the sacral with D and so on, up to the crown chakra, which connects with the B above middle C. In addition, vowel sounds and mantric words are used to aid connection with each chakra. Study the chart below if you would like to experiment with sound in relation to specific chakras.

PLANTS AND FLOWERS

Unless you dislike houseplants, try putting one or two in your own space. Because they are a 'living' energy, they can enhance the positive vibrations in your space and help you to relax. You will want to ensure that the plant has enough natural light. Fresh flowers are also an option. Many psychics always work with a vase of cut flowers next to them, choosing colours and scents that inspire them.

	CHAKRA	NOTE/TONE	VOWEL SOUND	MANTRA	CHAKRA SEED
1	BASE	C	UH	LAM	Lum
2	SACRAL	D	OOO	VAM	Vum
3	SOLAR PLEXUS	E	OH	RAM	Rum
4	HEART	F	AH	YAM	Yum/Sam
5	THROAT	G	EYE	HAM	Hum
6	THIRD EYE	A	AYE	AUM	Aum/Om
7	CROWN	B	EEE	AH	Ahh.../Aum

SCENTS

Scent is another important aspect to consider. What smells do you find appealing? Fresh lemons? Cinnamon? Lavender? Perhaps you prefer the smell of pine needles. Aromatherapy is an excellent way of developing your appreciation of scents, but please be aware that there are contra-indications medically which make using certain oils inadvisable, so check with your health practitioner before you use them.

You can also devise your own methods! Buy half a dozen lemons and place them in a wooden bowl to scent your room. If you like the smell of pine, take a walk in a pine forest and gather a handful of needles. Place them in a small dish. If a friend grows lavender, ask her or him for a few branches to tie and hang upside down to dry. The delicious smell of sweet lavender will fill your space for months. If geranium oil appeals to you, buy a small geranium plant with scented leaves, then simply press the leaves gently with your fingers to release the sweet perfume.

space every day. You can also purchase humidifiers to improve air quality. A simple way to keep the air 'fresh' is to purchase an inexpensive 'smudge stick', which is like a form of incense. You can find these in New Age or health shops.

There is also another simple technique you can try: put your hands together and clap vigorously as you move around your space. Pay particular attention to the corners. Does this sound odd? Try it and see. You might be amazed how different the energy feels afterwards – and clapping is free!

Whatever you decide to do in creating your personal space, remember you need to keep the energy flowing. Try moving objects around in your space and experiment with different colours, plants, scents and sounds. Make sure your space is kept clean. It's important that it grows and changes, encouraging growth and change in you.

TOUCH

You also need something pleasing to touch. What textures do you find comforting and enriching? For many people, it's something soft like silk or satin. Do you have a cushion you could place on your seat to touch as you start work? Perhaps you just have a small square of fabric that you like and want to keep on your chair. You will then imbue it with your energy and can use it as a means of recharging yourself quickly when you sit down to work. Have you noticed that in creating your own space, you have been giving thought to four of your five senses? Taste is the only one that isn't helpful to consider, as food and psychic study don't mix well.

FRESH AIR

Lastly, you need fresh air. If your space doesn't have its own window, make sure you can create a through draught so air can circulate freely. You should air your

CHAPTER FIVE:

Channelling Your Energy

In this chapter we are going to look at the benefits of breathing deeply and discover some further energy centres in our body. We shall also discuss how to channel the Universal and Earth energies effectively. Most importantly, we shall explore new techniques to cleanse, close down and protect ourselves, so no unwanted energies remain in our aura. Working at this deeper level, please remember to make sure you are free from any mind-altering substances and that no one disturbs you during the exercises.

DEEP BREATHING

Relaxation is vital for psychic development and the key to this is learning how to breathe deeply. The deeper and slower you breathe, the faster and smoother those cones of energy at your chakras will be whirring! Most of us don't make full use of our breath during our lifetime. Study the diagram below to see how breathing works. As much as possible, breathe air in through your nose rather than your mouth. Your nose contains tiny hairs and mucous membranes that help to filter out the impurities of the air. The nose also warms and moistens the air on its way to the lungs.

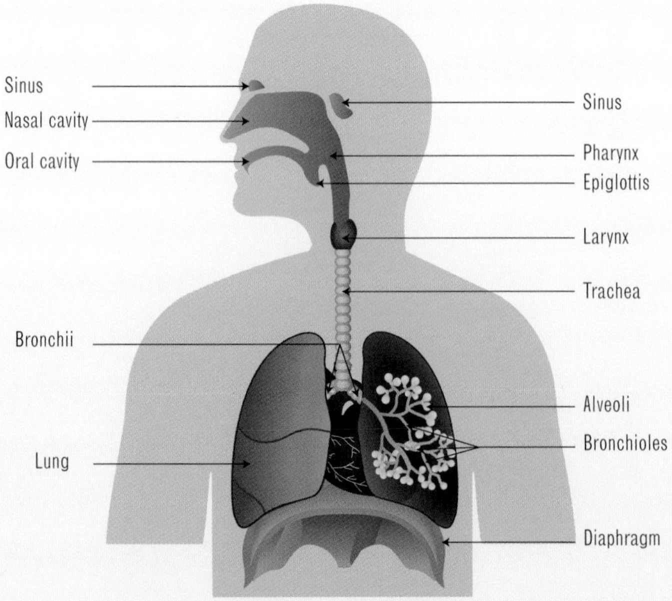

Once the air is drawn in through your nose, it travels down the larynx and into the trachea. The trachea then divides into two bronchii, which in turn each lead to a lung. Once the bronchus reaches the lung, it divides into smaller branches, called bronchioles. At the tip of each bronchiole are tiny balloon-like sacs called alveoli. Each lung contains nearly half a billion of these tiny sacs. If your breathing is always shallow, you never inflate all these tiny balloons and they start to deteriorate. The exchange of oxygen for carbon dioxide happens through minuscule blood vessels in the walls of the alveoli. (The pumping of the heart is then responsible for distributing the blood around the body via a complex web of blood vessels.) When we exhale, we release the carbon dioxide waste from our lungs.

THE DIAPHRAGM

The diaphragm plays a major role in controlling lung activity. It is a large, dome-shaped muscle lying directly under the lungs, which changes position as you breathe. When you inhale, the diaphragm stretches out and becomes almost flat, but when you exhale it curves into a deep upside-down 'U' shape to help push the unwanted air out of your lungs. The diaphragm is one of the most underused muscles in the human body and you will need to learn how to strengthen it in order to work psychically. Try the following exercise to check whether you're using your diaphragm properly.

Sinus
Nasal cavity
Oral cavity
Bronchii
Lung

Sinus
Pharynx
Epiglottis
Larynx
Trachea
Alveoli
Bronchioles
Diaphragm

EXERCISE – THE DIAPHRAGM

Stand up straight in front of a full-length mirror with your legs shoulder-width apart, and fix your eyes on your ribcage. Now place your hands gently over the base of your ribs, with your middle fingers barely touching. Try taking a comfortable breath in, but don't force it. Watch your ribcage as you do so. Is it expanding outwards, so that your fingertips are no longer touching? Exhale slowly. Do your fingertips meet again as you finish breathing out? Breathe in again gently to see if you can move your fingertips apart. Then exhale again. Are your fingers moving at all? Now breathe in again, but this time observe your shoulders. Are they lifting as you take your deep breath?

Most people find that their shoulders lift, but their fingertips barely move apart. This means they are shallow breathing, using the upper chest only. For psychic work it is important to learn how to strengthen the diaphragm muscle and deepen your breathing.

Now let your arms hang loosely by your side. Imagine that they have weights attached to them and notice how heavy they feel in their sockets. Make sure you don't slump as you do this. Think of the weights as grounding you, helping you to connect with the Earth energy, rather than forcing you into the ground. When your shoulders feel nice and heavy, lift your arms and place your fingers over your lower ribcage once more. Keep focused on how heavy and relaxed your shoulders feel. Now take another deeper breath. This time imagine your breath is going right down into your lower ribcage. Visualize it filling every part of you, nourishing and rejuvenating you. Has your ribcage moved outwards and have your fingertips moved just a little now? Practise this technique every day and you will notice a difference.

Alternatively, lie down to practise your diaphragm exercise. Lie flat on your back, placing a small pillow under your head and a slightly thicker one beneath your lower back. (This helps to open the ribcage.) Now practise deep breathing, with your hands resting lightly on your ribcage.

IMPORTANT!

All the exercises in this chapter need to be done gently when you first start. If you have never breathed deeply before you may quickly become dizzy. If at any time during the exercises you start to feel light-headed, immediately revert to your normal breathing until you feel grounded. Wait a few minutes before you try the exercise again.

EXERCISE – FILLING YOUR BODY WITH BREATH

For this exercise, you can either stand up straight, sit on a padded, upright chair or lie down on your back. Close your eyes and concentrate on your breathing. Start with gentle, comfortable breaths, gradually increasing their depth. As you breathe deeper, imagine the breath going deeper and deeper into your body. Imagine your lungs filled with warm, life-enriching air. Now imagine the breath is filling your shoulders, travelling down your arms and into your hands, filling up each finger right to the tip. As you breathe out, imagine the air filtering through your fingers. Now imagine the breath is going further into your body, filling your stomach with a warm sensation. Imagine the air is going through each thigh and knee joint, down each shin and into each foot, right to the tip of each toe. Then allow the breath to filter out through the toes. Now imagine each breath is filling every part of you and let each exhalation filter out through your fingertips and toes. Let the sensation of your breath fill every part of you. When you think of your hands, imagine every part of your palm and joint of every finger. The more specific you are, the more powerful the exercise will feel. Remember to return to your normal breathing before you open your eyes. Wait a few minutes before you do anything else.

If you watch someone sleeping, you will see that they are unconsciously breathing deeply. Their shoulders don't lift, but their chest and lower ribcage do. It seems that when we don't think about it and when we are truly relaxed, deep breathing becomes second nature to us. Practising your diaphragm development should be part of your daily fifteen-minute programme, even if it's only for a couple of minutes each time.

If you found the above exercise comfortable, you might want to move on to the one on the next page. This is even more powerful, as it focuses on the navel area, sometimes called the 'Hara'. A powerhouse of energy resides within the Hara.

EXERCISE — YOUR HARA AND UNIVERSAL ENERGY

Make sure you are seated for this exercise. Close your eyes and breathe gently. Place your hands lightly on your navel. How does that make you feel? Think about your navel, the importance of the umbilical card as you developed in the womb and the cutting of the cord when you were born.

As you do this, focus on the white Universal light which streams down from above and allow that pure light to come down through the top of your head and stream directly to your navel area. Feel the light pulsing under your hands as they rest on your navel. Focus your breath on that area until you are breathing the Universal energy in and out. Feel the intensity of the light increasing with every intake of breath.

Now become aware that the light is transferring itself to the tips of your fingers, through your navel. Your fingertips start to tingle and pulse in a pleasant way and you feel revitalized by the sensation.

If you have discomfort in another area of your body, you can transfer the energy via your fingers to help. Wait until you feel the power of the light tingling in your fingers then, after a deep inhalation, hold your breath and move your fingers to the part of your body that needs relaxation. Now exhale, feeling the energy of your fingers transferring deeply into that spot. Feel the energy disperse the discomfort. After you have exhaled completely, wait until you've returned your fingers to your navel before you inhale again. Repeat the process if you need to do so.

When you are ready to remove yourself from this exercise, focus on the weight of your body in the chair and the heaviness of your feet upon the floor. Use your image of roots growing from the soles of your feet to anchor you. Now pull the pink grounding Earth energy up from the centre of the Earth and feel it rise through your feet and legs and fill your navel area.

Stay focused on this Earth energy for a few moments before you open your eyes and reorientate yourself.

Both these exercises are useful to return to repeatedly, the first because it helps you fill your body with spiritually enriching breath and the second because you are working with the flow of Universal light, guiding it safely through your body. These exercises become more powerful when you repeat them regularly.

NADIS – ENERGY CHANNELS

Now we're going to look at balancing energy in a slightly different way. You may already be familiar with the idea of balance in the form of positive–negative, yin–yang, man–woman and sun–moon relationships. You can find that dual-power pull within the composition of the atom, in every cell and in the polarity of the Earth. This negative–positive power is also present within our own bodies in the form of 'nadis'.

Nadis are thin electrical currents or very fine energy channels through which our energy flows. The principle of the nadis is the same as that of any electrical current: the negative, positive and earth wires. It is generally believed that there are at least 72,000 tiny, thin lines running around and through our bodies, crisscrossing in every direction. Fortunately, to understand how to balance the male and female parts of ourselves, we need only to look at three major energy channels. These are:

1 The Sushumna – the main, earth nadi, which runs vertically through the spine, connecting all seven chakras.
2 The Ida – the female, negative nadi, which spirals up from the left of the base chakra, winding itself round the Sushumna to culminate in the left side of the brain.
3 The Pingala – the male, positive nadi, which spirals up from the right of the base chakra, winding itself around the Sushumna to culminate in the right side of the brain.

A useful symbol expressing this configuration of energy is the wand of Hermes, which is also known as the Caduceus.

You can learn how to balance these three energies so that they take you further along your path to enlightenment. The exercise on the next page is a form of yoga and is extremely powerful when done properly. Initially it might feel odd and uncomfortable since it can be difficult to hold your breath for the length of time suggested. If so, reduce the number of seconds for each section and gradually increase them again when you become more proficient. Although the exercise is described using the right hand, you can use either hand. If you have sinus problems you won't be able to follow this exercise. You need two clear nostrils to benefit from it.

EXERCISE – ALTERNATE NOSTRIL BREATHING

Hold your right hand up to your face with the palm towards you. Now place your thumb gently against your right nostril so that, in a moment, you'll be able to close off the airflow into that nostril. Place your third (or ring) finger over your left nostril, ready to do the same. Place your index and second fingers so that they rest gently against the third eye chakra at your forehead or, if you prefer, fold them into your palm as shown in the photo. It is sometimes said that by placing your two fingers against the third eye chakra you increase the spiritual power of this exercise. Try both and decide for yourself. Now lightly close your right nostril and breathe in slowly through your left nostril, for a count of four. Now close both nostrils and hold for a count of four. Release your right nostril and breathe out through that for a count of four. Without interrupting the flow, breathe in again through the right nostril, for a count of four. Close both nostrils and hold for four seconds. Release your left nostril and breathe out again through that nostril. Repeat this process five more times. Here's a quick recap of the order:

1. Breathe in through left nostril for four seconds.
2. Keep both nostrils closed for four seconds.
3. Breathe out through right nostril for four seconds.
4. Without stopping, breathe in through right nostril for four seconds.
5. Keep both nostrils closed for four seconds.
6. Breathe out through left nostril for four seconds.

As soon as you have got into the rhythm, you will find it easy to maintain a smooth flow. Gradually increase the number of seconds until you can manage ten seconds on each side. This won't be possible immediately as you will make yourself dizzy unless you build up to it slowly over a few months. Again, this exercise should be done every day. When you have developed a regular flow of breathing and can do five or six sets of the exercise without pausing, you will really notice a difference. It's not one you can easily put into words but you will feel yourself regaining a sense of balance. Both halves of you will seem more equal in weight and size. It isn't until you finish the exercise that you can appreciate how unbalanced you were before you started it!

Many of the exercises in this chapter are used in yoga. If you have the opportunity to take a yoga class, it can greatly increase your spiritual awareness and aid psychic development. There is an old yogic proverb which says:

'Life is in the breath; therefore he who only half-breathes, half lives.'

OTHER BENEFITS

It's also worth pointing out that awareness of breath can help you relax in many ways, apart from developing your inner psychic. Focus on your breathing whenever you feel nervous or angry; feel the steady rhythm calm and ground you. If you get hiccups, stop to focus on breathing slowly and deeply and imagine your breath releasing the airlock in your stomach – it really works!

You may often have been told in the past, 'Count to ten before you speak', but now, instead of simply counting to ten, use the time to concentrate on your breath. The more you remember the power of breathing, the more it will help you in all you do.

Now we move on to the process of opening up and learning how to cleanse, close and protect ourselves. These are crucial exercises because you need to use them every time you work with your inner psychic. It's a good idea to read through them several times to get a clear sense of what is involved before you start.

Your carefully created personal space is vital to this process because you need to feel safe, relaxed and calm. Ensure that your phone is switched off and no one can disturb you. Once you are ready, sit on your padded, upright chair and slowly let yourself be guided through the exercise on the following pages.

EXERCISE – OPENING UP

Start by focusing on the weight of your body in the chair. Do you feel evenly balanced on both sides of your body? One side of the body usually holds more tension than the other. Do a few rounds of alternate nostril breathing before you continue. Remember the power of your Ida and Pingala nadis as they coil around your Sushumna, the central 'rod' through which all your chakras connect. Imagine these three nadis and feel them glowing with energy inside you.

Now concentrate on deepening your breathing, without forcing it. Become aware of each intake of breath and how it caresses the inside of your body. Enjoy the release as you exhale. If you feel any aches or twinges in your body, take a breath in and try to send that breath to the spot where the pain is, using it to disperse the discomfort. As you breathe out, take the ache with it and release it into the distance. Feel your ribcage expand with each breath and enjoy the sense of freedom it allows. Try not to raise your shoulders as you breathe, but let them feel heavy and relaxed. Spend a moment focusing on your diaphragm and becoming aware of how it is flat as you breathe in and then arches up as you breathe out; it feels comfortable and fluid in movement.

Now tune in to the edges of your aura. Where are they today? How far from your body? Using the technique you learned on page 47, gently expand your aura. Breathe in and feel it expand, breathe out and feel it settle. Stop once you feel comfortable with your aura's expansion.

Next start to visualize a beautiful, pure, bright, white light streaming into the centre of the room from above you. Feel the warmth and brightness of this Universal energy; let it become strong and powerful. It's there, always there, and by visualizing it you make it stronger all the time. Allow the light to come closer, to come down into the room and circle you. Fill the whole room with that beautiful light energy. Keep remembering that the more you focus on the Universal energy, the stronger it becomes. Depending on your spiritual/ religious beliefs, you may want to give thanks to its source, before you continue.

Now visualize this pure white light coming down through your crown chakra. This is a chakra that's always open, remember, so you can just let the light enter you and slowly filter through your body, gently cleansing and rejuvenating each part of you. Let the light trickle through you like a warm shower: through your head, neck, shoulders, arms and hands, then let it run out through your fingers. Now let

it run through the rest of your body: chest, ribcage, stomach, all the vertebrae of your back, then through your hips, legs and down into your feet, then let it filter out through your toes, taking any tension or worries with it. Repeat this process several times, enjoying the sensation of muscles and joints relaxing, of cares and problems washing out of you. Always bring in the light as you breathe in and feel the tension trickling out through your fingers and toes on each exhalation of breath.

Now concentrate on your feet as they rest on the floor. Imagine the soles of your feet with roots growing down into the ground, feeling secure and safe. Then visualize the pink Earth energy coming up through the ground and into the soles of your feet. This grounding energy comes from deep within the Earth's core and connects you to everything on our planet. Stretch your toes and feel this Earth energy coming through into them. Remember to use your breathing to help the visualization and, with each breath in, slowly draw the energy up through your body. Think of each part of your body, each muscle and joint, and work your way up the body to your shoulders. Then let the Earth energy flow down your arms and hands and out through your fingers. Now let the Earth energy flow from your shoulders and up through your neck and into your head, feeling it meet the pure white Universal light at your crown and blend with it. Now that you are fully experiencing the dual flow of Universal energy and Earth energy and allowing your deep breathing to fill all of you, you are ready to open your chakras.

Start with the first, the base chakra, located at the bottom of your spine. Remember the cone of this energy centre opens downwards to the ground and is always open, although we need to speed it up or open it more fully. This sensation of opening is different for everyone and you can use various visualization techniques to help you. Imagine it is an electric fan that has been revolving very slowly and you are turning up the speed. Imagine the four petals of a beautiful red flower unfolding. Picture a drawbridge or a door slowly

opening or a parcel being unwrapped – or use another image that works for you. Try murmuring the name 'muladhara' (moo-lahd-harr-rah) and remember it means 'root'. This chakra is about your right to be here in the physical world.

As you focus and the base chakra opens more fully, you may experience a sensation like the flutter of butterfly wings, or a tingle, a warmth or a twirling sensation. In the beginning you may feel nothing. If at any time while opening the chakras you feel uncomfortable, simply use the light to cleanse yourself. Cleanse yourself as often as you like. The base chakra is red so, as you open the centre, imagine the colour red. Don't just think of the colour, imagine it all around you and in you; feel the colour, feel its richness and vibration. Use a symbol if it helps.

Now move up to the second chakra, which is the sacral chakra, located just below your navel. This opens front and back, so you need to imagine two centres opening. Use your thought process to make them open for you. Remember your orange flower with the six petals. See both cones whirring into action. Softly say the name 'swadisthana' (svah-dist-tana) and remember this means 'sacred home of the self' and is about your ability to create intimacy with others. Then think of the colour orange and fill yourself with it, front and back. If, during your concentration, you start to shallow breathe, draw your attention back to your breathing to deepen it again. If any emotions or sensations you don't like come to you as the sacral chakra opens, wash them away with the Universal light. As this chakra opens, notice if you have a different sensation when the two cones start to whirr. Sometimes the cones opening feel different at different chakras. As your connection with your cones strengthens, you will appreciate their subtle differences.

Next concentrate on the solar plexus, which is above and to the left of the navel. This also opens front and back, so use your preferred method of visualization to open the two cones. In the beginning, try a different thought process each time and then discover what is most powerful for you. Picture your beautiful ten-petalled yellow flower and let the sunshine yellow colour fill your solar plexus area. Softly whisper the word 'manipura' (man-ee-pooh-rah) and know this means 'city of jewels'. This chakra is about your purpose in life and your willpower. If it helps you to connect by gently touching your solar plexus chakra openings, then do so. If you have any sensation you don't like, let the Universal light flow through you and wash it away.

Now we move to the heart chakra, above the chest in the middle. Open its drawbridge or petals or switch on the fan and start opening the heart's energy centre, front and back. See the cones open and start to whirr. Your green flower has twelve petals. Murmur 'anahata' (ah-nah-hah-ta) which means 'unstruck sound' and remember that this is the level at which your chakra energies become finer and lighter. The heart chakra is the bridge between the physical and spiritual world and it's where we embrace unconditional love. You may find the sensation of opening start to change here. It's very hard to describe until you experience it, but you are now moving onto a higher vibration and it may feel finer and lighter. If you feel nothing different, don't dwell on that, just continue opening up. Once you can see the colour green clearly, draw it into your heart centre both front and back and let that warm, loving colour fill you completely. When you feel filled with the green light of love and compassion, move on.

Next is the throat chakra at the hollow of the throat. Front and back, open the centres and experience your own tingle or whirring or butterfly tickle. As we move higher, the sensation will become lighter and finer still. Your cones of energy will whirr at a faster speed. Your blue flower has sixteen petals. Now softly say the word 'vishuddha' (vee-shoo-duh) meaning 'pure place'. This chakra is about our self-expression, particularly in relation to how we listen to and express higher truths. Tune in to the colour of sky blue. Imagine the limitless expanse of a clear blue sky. Let the cooling, inspirational colour of sky blue now come into your body, front and back, and fill every part of you.

Then make your way up your body to your third eye, in the middle of your forehead. This also opens front and back, so start your process of opening, again always remembering to keep breathing. It's very easy to stop altogether for a moment as you concentrate on opening and creating colours, so keep checking that you are letting your body breathe all the time. The third eye energy centre is purple, and this time your beautiful purple flower has only two big petals or 'wings'. Open those wings and allow the vibrant colour purple to flow through your energy centres, front and back. Whisper the word 'ajna' (arg-nya) and know it means 'beyond wisdom'. This chakra is also called your perception centre, so this is where your intuition and connection to higher realms manifests itself. What will you allow yourself to receive here in future? Your third eye cones are whirring on such a fine, high speed now, it is hard to see them, but you know they are there and open.

Now focus on your crown chakra, the highest vibration of the chakra energies. Remember this centre, like the base, is always open but we need to open it further. The cone of this energy centre is outside your physical body, a few centimetres above the crown of your head. Open those flower petals or that door or increase the whirring fan's speed. Your white flower has thousands of petals this time, reflecting the higher consciousness accessed here and the infinite opportunities for enlightenment. The word you want to whisper very softly here, or speak silently in your mind, is 'sahasrara' (suh-huss-rah-rah) which means 'infinite'. You may not be able to see the cone of energy whirring here because it is so light and fine, but

you know it is there and part of your higher self. Repeat the word several times. This centre opens upwards to the sky, reaching to the infinite Universal energy. You may find your body straightening as you focus on the crown chakra, as though your own energy is being lifted up and connecting with the light above.

When you are ready, pull the pure Universal energy down into you again, this time feeling the difference as it flows through all your chakras, which are now fully open and whirring at their individual speeds. You may find this a powerful experience and the sensation may leave you feeling very uplifted and a little 'buzzy'.

If you feel heady or off-balance, you need to concentrate your energies back to earth. To do this, think only of your feet and concentrate all your energies on them. Imagine long, deep roots growing out of your feet and anchoring you deep into the ground. Feel how heavy your feet are and think of the floor and how it feels under you.

EXERCISE – LIFTING AND LOWERING ENERGIES

Once you have opened up, you need to be able to lift and lower your energies through your chakras in order to 'use' your inner psychic. The more time you spend practising this process, the more effective you will be in your psychic readings.

Imagine that each chakra is a different floor in a building and your energies are in a lift, which you are going to 'take' to various floors. The lift is your Sushumna, the nadi, or rod of energy, which connects all your chakras. The base chakra is your ground floor, the sacral the first floor, the solar plexus the second, and so on. Remember that at this point you will only be lifting energies as far as the third floor, your heart chakra. To go any higher at this stage of your journey would be confusing.

First of all you want to practise lifting your energy from your base (ground floor) to your sacral (first floor). As you breathe in, imagine the energy within you is shooting up in a lift and reaching that first floor. When you breathe out, your lift stops at the first floor. For some people, this is a very strong feeling; it can be possible to have the energy shoot straight up your Sushumna and go further up your chakras. You will know if this has happened because you will feel a bolt of energy racing up through your body – a bit as though you have been wired to an electricity supply! If this happens, focus immediately on the pink Earth energy and draw it up all through you. Focus on the roots growing from the soles of your feet. Make sure you feel well grounded before you try again. For other people, the sensation is hardly discernible. There isn't a right way or a wrong way to experience this, it will be personal to you.

Now try lifting your energies to the second floor and finally to the third floor, your heart chakra. Take your time and observe what sensations you experience as you do this. What is the speed of your lift? Is it smooth or a bit creaky and jerky? What do you feel inside when your lift moves? What you will soon realize is that your energy always wants to return quite quickly to your base chakra: the default switch on your lift seems to be the ground floor! Therefore, when you work psychically, one of your main roles is to remember to keep lifting your energies up through your body in your psychic lift and learning how to control your lift at a speed and level that suits you.

When you feel you have spent enough time lifting and lowering your energies, move straight to the cleansing and closing exercises on the next page.

IMPORTANT!

Before you try to pick up anything psychically while lifting and lowering your energies, you must first practise the cleansing and closing down processes. This is most important. It is necessary because at any time during initial psychic work you may feel uncomfortable or you might pick up on someone else's discomfort and take on board their symptoms for a while. This is harmless, as long as you cleanse and re-energize.

If you have opened up properly, you will understand why this is important. You will probably feel very good, still slightly 'up in the air' and extremely aware of everything around you. If you inadvertently open your eyes at any point during the opening-up process, the room may appear much brighter, richer. It may even have a resonance you weren't aware of before; your senses feel heightened and sharpened. All this is wonderful: congratulations! Allow yourself a moment to acknowledge what you have accomplished before you close your eyes again and start the cleansing process.

CLEANSING AND CLOSING DOWN

Before you close down all the chakras, you need to ensure you are not leaving anything unwelcome inside you. Once you start working properly with others, you will be pulling outside influences into your own aura. You have to do this to enable you to 'read' your subject and use your psychic abilities. So let's practise getting rid of those effects.

EXERCISE – CLEANSING

There is more than one technique you can use, so let's look at a few and you can decide which one works best for you.

UNIVERSAL ENERGY CLEANSING

First, you can use the bright white Universal light coming through the top of your crown chakra and feel it wash all through you – but this time be aware of any residue you may still have inside. Did something you pick up disturb you, unbalance you, or cause mild pain or emotional hurt? You must be aware of your body, tune in to what it is saying and then consciously let unwanted energy go. As you breathe in the white light, direct it to wherever you feel off-balance (quite often it's around the solar plexus and sacral areas, our emotional centres) and really concentrate on washing the feeling away. Remember you need to focus on your breathing first, then concentrate on the Universal light above you and draw it down into your body, directing it specifically to where you feel discomfort. You can repeat this process as many times as you like until you feel 'clean'.

A WATERFALL

Alternatively you can imagine the white Universal light as a cool, comforting waterfall and feel the water trickling into your body and through your whole system, giving you a good psychic wash inside! Once you've practised this a few times, it becomes an easy and very comforting part of the process.

YOUR CLEANSING SANCTUARY

You can take this waterfall image a step further and create your own waterfall in an idyllic setting in your mind; picture yourself stepping under the waterfall as you do so. Or perhaps you have a dream of the perfect shower in a perfect bathroom? Create whatever stimulates your imagination and makes you feel good, then put yourself within that picture. The stronger and more vivid your visualization, the more comforting and healing the cleansing process becomes. You should always be alone in your cleansing sanctuary as it is your own very private space. Always remember to let the residue water or light spill out of your fingers and toes, never leave any inside you. Inhale the light or waterfall and release it through your fingers and toes on the exhalation.

Developing a powerful cleansing technique is also useful for everyday life. You know when you step off a crowded, smelly train, having felt almost suffocated by everyone else's aura? Take a moment to 'cleanse' then. Even try using it while you're squashed in the train! Create your own psychic space and step into the waterfall. The great thing about using your imagination is that no one else knows what you're doing. There are so many times in our everyday lives when outside stress comes crowding in on us: visiting someone who is unwell, trying to calm a fractious child or bad-tempered person, dealing with a demanding client at work, being stuck in a traffic jam or feeling sick before facing a daunting task. On all these occasions, cleansing your body and aura is an invaluable tool to help you cope. The more you practise it, the more powerful it will become.

Closing down is as important as the cleansing process because, unless you protect your aura as you finish psychic work, you will continue, even unconsciously, to pick up further energies from people. Don't start this process until you have cleansed properly.

If you are working with another person through all these exercises, do make sure you give them the space to create what works for them. You may well both have very different images for opening and closing chakras, visualizing colours, cleansing and protecting yourselves.

EXERCISE – CLOSING DOWN

Once you feel psychically 'scrubbed clean', using whatever technique works best for you, focus on how much your aura has expanded during your opening-up process. If you have been practising aura awareness in everyday life, you'll sense how much wider it feels now. You need to retract it again. Concentrate first of all on how large it feels. Where are its outer edges: a metre, a metre-and-a-half away? As you take in a breath, feel your aura suck inwards, closer to you. As you breathe out, let your aura settle. Once it feels comfortable around you, stop.

Now you need to go through the chakras, one by one, closing each down. You don't need to use the colours for this shutting-down process, as focusing on the colours can make the chakras want to stay open! Again, start with the base chakra and concentrate on its location at the base of the spine. This one is always open but we've revved it up to spin much faster than normal so now we have to slow it down. Use the reverse process of what you used before: fold up all the flower petals until they close into one another, pull up the drawbridge, close the door or turn the fan down to low. Depending on how well you opened it in the first place, that is, how fast your energy centre is spinning, it may take a few moments for you to control its speed and slow it down. You must always be in control during psychic work, so practise that control now by making the chakra spin more slowly.

Once you are satisfied that it really has slowed down, you may wish to psychically 'seal' the centre with a circle of light and a cross. It might help if you imagine a psychic pen with a nib of pure light. Use that pen to draw a circle and then a cross. This can be helpful because once you start putting all these exercises together and fully opening up you may feel more vulnerable than you expected. Once you really focus on your chakras, they become a very 'real' and vibrant part of you. They are very much gateways into the heart of who and what you are, so it's understandable that once they are open, you may feel a little exposed. Lifting and lowering the energies along your Sushumna, your psychic lift, further activates the chakras. Using your psychic pen to seal and protect them as you close down may be a comforting tool for you, particularly in the early stages.

Now work your way up the chakras. Can you remember their order? Base, sacral, solar plexus, heart, throat, third eye and crown. Use the same process but remember the middle five must all be closed completely. This may make it easier for you: imagine the centres utterly still and closed, sealed with a circle and a cross. The crown, like the base, is always open, but because it will have opened much more during your work, you must take time to slow it down.

If, once you have closed all seven chakras, you still feel a little 'up in the air', cleanse again with the white light or your waterfall/shower room. You can never cleanse too much! If you don't feel grounded properly, use your feet anchored to the floor as your guide. Imagine them with long, strong roots into the ground and feel how heavy they are. Use the beautiful pink Earth energy and pull it into you. After a few minutes, your energies should be well grounded again.

To test this, slowly open your eyes. Does the room feel 'brighter' than usual? Do objects around you seem to be pulsing with energy? Then you aren't closed down! Close your eyes and repeat your method of closing down your chakras. Then spend more time connecting with the grounding Earth energy. Open your eyes and make sure everything around you feels 'normal' before you continue with your day. It is always good to drink a glass of water when you finish, so get into the habit of having one by your chair before you start.

EXERCISE — YOUR PSYCHIC CLOAK

As a last protective measure, you should draw a psychic 'cloak' up around you to make you feel secure and safe. Again, there are various ways of doing this. Some like to see it as a sheath of warm light coming up and around them; others use an image of fabric (think of something soft, like wool or silk, which feels good against your skin); some imagine an enormous, warm, fluffy towel enveloping them securely. Pick your own image, but make sure the colour you use is light, not dark. A dark colour could leave you feeling low in energy, as dark colours absorb the light. It might help you to imagine the cloak rising up from your feet and gradually coming up over your whole body as high as your neck. If you still feel 'open', then imagine a zipper or buttons or Velcro to do up the front and/or back to make you feel even more secure. You might even want it to have a hood to draw up over your head when you need it. Experiment with what feels right for you.

This cloak is something you can use whenever you feel vulnerable, not just when you are consciously working with your inner psychic. It is part of your energetic armour and can be a great comfort. The more you use it, the more 'real' it becomes and the more effective it will be in protecting you. Whenever you are in a situation that is making you feel uncomfortable, throw your psychic cloak around you.

SELF-PROTECTION

A final word about opening up and closing down. As a beginner, never practise 'opening up' in public, but feel free to practise closing down at any time. The reason for this is that we can open up quite easily under certain circumstances and not realize it. A sudden rush of love can open our heart chakra or an impassioned speech will open our throat centre, but we seldom think of closing ourselves down again. When you start working with your inner psychic, it is very exciting. Even by talking animatedly to friends about what you have done, you can start opening the chakras without realizing it. When you finish talking, you need to close down again. Remember only to open up under safe, controlled circumstances.

EXERCISE – YOUR INNER SELF

Settle yourself comfortably in your space and close your eyes. Open up in your own time, without rushing. Wait until you feel relaxed and ready to work, and keep your eyes closed throughout this exercise.

You discover you are walking in a garden of your dreams. Everything is perfect – it's exactly as you want it to be. Walk slowly through the garden, admiring everything you love – flowers, trees, shrubs, a pond, a lake, ducks, squirrels, birds. Hear the birdsong, feel the warm sun on your head. As you walk along, you see a gate in front of you. It's a wonderful gate that looks inviting. You open it up and walk through. In front of you, you see a building. It's your image of a perfect place to be. As you approach, you see a key in the door.

You turn the key. The door opens and you step inside. The interior is decorated exactly as you want it to be. It's comfortable and welcoming, furnished with everything you love most. The colours are perfect for you. The smell and light and space feel exactly right.

You sit down in the middle of your wonderful abode and close your eyes. Very soon, you hear a voice calling you. It sounds soft and welcoming. This is your inner self. Acknowledge its presence and ask for its help. Explain that you want to get to know it better. Ask advice on how you may do this. Hear how loving and wise the voice is as it replies. Feel nurtured and safe as it speaks. Enter into a gentle dialogue together.

When it is time, the voice tells you that you must leave. It also lets you know that you can return again when you wish to do so. You thank the voice for its guidance and wisdom. Then you slowly get up and make your way to the door. As you turn around for one last look at your private sanctuary, you see there is a gift for you in the centre of the room. This is personal to you. It is for you to meditate upon; it's related to the discussion you have just been having with your inner self. Take the gift with you.

As you leave, close the door behind you and turn the key in the lock. Return to the gate and go through into the garden, closing the gate behind you. Walk back through your heavenly garden, holding your gift in your hands, until you return to where you started.

Now you are back in your seat again, with your eyes closed. Think about what your inner self told you and why your gift was important. Then use the waterfall or light to cleanse through all your thoughts. Make yourself feel empty and clean again. Go through the closing-down process thoroughly and ground yourself with the Earth energy. Concentrate on your feet for several minutes before you open your eyes again. If when you open your eyes the room feels very bright and full of energy, close them and repeat the closing-down process.

The early stages of psychic discovery are about building your confidence and learning what works for you. Discovering your inner psychic also entails delving into who you are in a profound and meaningful way – as you may be realizing from your experiences during these recent exercises! The exercise above, which is a gentle meditation, may help you gain insight into your personal spirituality.

This is a meditation you can return to whenever you feel the need. It is a good way to get in touch with your inner self. After a while, you may not need to go through your garden and into your sanctuary to make contact, but it will help you to do so initially.

Were you surprised by some of the things you were told? Or did you feel that part of you knew them already? Trust your inner voice. Listen to it whenever you can. Always ask for its help. It's part of the higher you and it is meant to be used. Trust it. Believe in it.

During psychic work, you need to become an instrument through which energies can flow.

WORKING ON YOURSELF

During psychic work, you need to become an instrument through which energies can flow. If your own energies are perfectly balanced with the Universal and Earth energies, if your psychic lift is always well oiled and works smoothly and easily, you become a powerful instrument that resonates in perfect harmony. You then become a good transmitter of information. The more balance you can create, the better you will be as a psychic tool.

So you need to work on yourself when you're alone, when psychic development is not in your thoughts, when you're looking at how you relate to everything and everyone around you. You need to look at the areas of your life that aren't working and be willing to delve into the bits of you that make you feel uncomfortable, and learn why. You have to learn how to release pent-up, destructive emotions and clear blocks. You are then learning how to make your own energies flow harmoniously. You never stop learning how to do this.

You could use the image of making yourself into an empty vessel, free from stagnant thoughts or anxieties. The more you can clear any blocks within you and the more empty you can make yourself, the better you will feel in all aspects of your life. When we say empty, it doesn't mean without energy, of course! Empty just means devoid of earthly

constraints and challenges, freeing yourself so that all your spiritual energy flows unhindered through you, allowing you to interact with the Universal and Earth energies in the most uninhibited way.

Before you move on to the next chapter, check that you feel comfortable with everything you have experienced during the exercises in this section because we have covered a lot! These are the major concepts you need to understand:

- the importance of breathing deeply and how to do this
- the role of the diaphragm and how you can strengthen this muscle
- the significance of the Sushumna, Ida and Pingala nadis
- alternate nostril breathing
- the Hara energy centre at your navel and how to tune in to it
- the opening-up process
- the importance of your psychic lift and how to operate it
- the different cleansing processes
- the closing-down process and your psychic pen
- the importance of your psychic cloak
- your willingness to work on your spiritual growth.

CHAPTER SIX:

Your First Sitting

This short but vital chapter looks at how to choose appropriate people upon whom you can practise initially, so that you can offer effective readings even at this early stage. It will encourage you to think about your personal responsibilities to your sitter. It can be exciting when you first start picking up information about other people and you will no doubt want to be as helpful as possible. At the same time it is easy to say the wrong thing by accident or to phrase something badly without realizing you are doing so. Here are some basic dos and don'ts to help you to give safe readings and ensure that you and your sitter finish in a positive and comfortable frame of mind.

CHOOSING THE RIGHT SITTER

Now that you've reached the stage when you can start practising, your next step is to find someone upon whom you can practise! If you've worked alone so far, this is when you need to find a person who is happy to be your guinea pig. It is best that you don't already know a great deal about your prospective sitter, so that you aren't tempted to talk about aspects of their life with which you are familiar. You may feel daunted by the thought of working with someone you don't know well, but it puts less pressure on you to prove yourself with a stranger than with a close friend.

You may be wondering how you will possibly find someone suitable, but it isn't as difficult as it sounds. Once you start talking to people about wanting to increase your psychic abilities, you'll discover that almost everyone has some interest in the phenomenon. Indifference is rare in this field. If you can summon up the confidence to talk about your psychic work, you will start to discover quite a few people who say they're happy to be experimented upon!

You need to stress to your prospective sitter that, as a beginner, you can't guarantee positive results, although you will be doing your best! It's also important that you appreciate and acknowledge the time they are giving you. When people feel appreciated, they are even more willing to bear with you as you work your way through the early stages.

MAKING YOUR SITTER FEEL COMFORTABLE

Sitters who come to you for the first time probably won't know what is going to happen, so it's up to you to put them at their ease. The more relaxed they are, the easier it will be for you to pick up information. Make sure your sitter is seated in a comfortable chair and check they're not hot or cold or thirsty. All these factors affect the atmosphere in the room.

The first thing is to manage the sitter's expectations, because people often associate psychic work with contacting loved ones who have passed on. It's important they realize straightaway that this is not what you do. Let them know that you will be picking up personal information about them and things that are happening in their life. If you want to go into a little more detail, you could say that you will be tuning into their energy, or aura, and hopefully picking up information they will find useful or uplifting.

Explain that you will take a few minutes to tune in by sitting quietly and concentrating on your breathing. Also remind them that this session is just experimental and you can't guarantee results, but you hope that you will provide something useful. Tell them you will start to speak as you sense or see things and ask them to respond mainly with a 'yes' or 'no'. They may be anxious to tell you about themselves, but if they do it reduces your ability to pick things up for yourself. Explain this to them and ask them to keep detailed comments to themselves until the end of the sitting. Tell them that they don't have to be thinking or trying to 'give out' anything to you. It's a common mistake for people to make, putting psychic work into the realms of telepathy or ESP. You are tuning in to them and they don't have to do a thing, apart from to relax as much as possible. Always, at the beginning or end of the session (or both), thank them for their assistance.

Once you have experimented with a few people, you will appreciate how different we all are: some people will be very closed and hard to penetrate; others will seem to have information pouring out of them; some will fill you with a warm glow as you interpenetrate their aura; others will throw you off balance. (Remember to use your alternate nostril breathing and ground yourself with the pink Earth energy if this happens!) It's a fascinating process as you discover how truly individual humans are. Psychic work affords us concrete proof of that.

YOUR RESPONSIBILITIES

When you first start receiving information psychically, it is incredibly exciting and almost impossible not to tell your sitter immediately everything you are seeing and sensing. However, you must give consideration to the way you do this; always stop to think about what you're going to say before you say it. Here are a few examples to demonstrate why this is so necessary:

1 You've tuned in to your sitter and suddenly, after a few moments, an image flashes across your mind. You're thrilled, of course – something is happening! You say quickly, 'A coffin. I see a coffin!' Can you imagine what that image might mean to your sitter? They may have a friend or relative who's ill and immediately assume that they're going to die. Or they may have a terrible fear of death (many people do) and think that they're the one about to die. To you, the coffin may have seemed perfectly innocent, covered in beautiful flowers perhaps. Perhaps it symbolizes an emotion – the person letting go of a problem or saying goodbye to an unhappy relationship, for example. But you just said 'a coffin'.

2 You've tuned in and suddenly you feel a twinge in your stomach and say, 'There's something wrong in your stomach area. I sense a pain there.' The way most people are programmed is to fear the worst – an illness (often cancer), an operation, or something terrible that will adversely affect their lives. That pain you picked up on might have been an emotional one: perhaps the person feels as if they are emotionally being 'kicked in the gut' by someone, or they are worried about an upcoming project at work, or perhaps they just have butterflies in their stomach because they are your first sitter! But you just said, 'There's something wrong in your stomach area.'

3 You've tuned in and picked up on your sitter's concern about their mother. You say, 'Your mother's unwell and you're worried about her.' Your sitter might then think you're implying that her condition will worsen or they might even say, 'Yes, that's true, but her problem isn't serious.' You think nothing of it and carry on. Then your sitter returns home and spends days worrying about their mother before she finally recovers her health. You gave your sitter needless stress by your casual remark: 'Your mother's unwell.'

4 You see in your mind's eye a dark tunnel ahead, or you receive an image where you move from the light into the dark. This image makes a strong impression on you, so you say, 'I see darkness,' or 'There is a dark tunnel now.' To you, the tunnel might represent a period of calm or peace after a busy time or you might feel it is exciting because there is some unexpected journey ahead for this person – but you just said, 'I see darkness.'

You may think it unlikely you'd ever be as insensitive as this, but the truth is that you will probably be even more so unless you stop to think first. When you're excited, it's difficult to consider how to phrase things, but it's one of your most important jobs. Returning to the examples above, here's how you could have chosen your words to avoid alarm:

1 It's never wise to mention a symbol such as a coffin, gun or knife – or any object which might be construed as threatening – because people won't understand its meaning unless you elaborate on it. Instead, ask yourself what the symbol is 'saying' to you, then phrase your sentence along the lines of: 'I feel something or someone was troubling you, but you have now let it go,' or 'I feel as if something has been metaphorically stabbing you in the back recently and you want to do something about

it,' or 'I feel that someone may be shooting down your confidence right now and you want to deal with that.' There are many ways to interpret the symbols you receive, but this analysis can only come with practice and, until you can work with it and understand it, it's important to choose your words carefully. If you are in doubt about the images you see, don't mention anything that might be distressing, just cleanse yourself and move on to the next image.

2 Physical pains are tricky to figure out, but if you feel that whatever you pick up on is on a physical rather than an emotional level, phrase your comments something like this: 'It feels as though something has affected your tummy area recently, does that make sense to you?' If the sitter offers a 'yes' response or admits to something similar, then cleanse yourself of the feeling before moving on. If you feel it may not be a physical pain, but a related emotional one, then try to tune in on that level and offer an appropriate comment, such as, 'I think you have a gut feeling that someone around you isn't treating you properly and you want

to rectify that,' or 'I feel you're very nervous about some ongoing project in your life.'

3 If the information you are getting suggests your sitter is unwell, this is a very difficult situation. It's vital for you to realize that at no point should you give advice on anything medical, as it would be dangerous for you to do so. What you might want to do is offer some comfort. For instance, you might feel your sitter is worrying so much that they are making themselves worse. Or they may be feeling guilty when they've no need to do so. Or they might be troubled by a lack of communication in their relationship with their mother, or whoever, which they see as a state of being unwell. You need to be clear about what you want to say before you speak. If all you can see is that someone is unwell, but you get no further information, then cleanse yourself and move on.

4 Many people may be alarmed by images of darkness or dark tunnels. They might think of death or of hidden traumas to come. Of course, these images may just mean peace and solitude and many other positive things, but your sitter won't know that unless you explain. So if you pick up anything to do with darkness, either avoid mentioning it or make sure you can translate it into a context that is comfortable and reassuring, such as: 'I can see some moments of peace and calm ahead for you.'

CLOSING A READING

Make sure you always close the sitting with a positive statement. Your sitter is likely to remember your final words, which may stay with them for quite a while. It's important that your sitter leaves feeling uplifted, not depressed. They are giving you their time, free of charge, and they deserve to have a pleasant experience. (The added bonus is that it will also make them feel more inclined to sit for you again!) This does not mean you should lie to your sitter and exaggerate something simply to make them feel good. It just means you need to concentrate on the positive.

By all means offer thought-provoking comments during the reading, but never leave your sitter in a confused or sad state. You should always check this before they leave because you might not realize that something you said has worried or thrown them. When in doubt, ask them more than once if they have any more questions or if anything has left them confused. Tell them, no matter how silly it seems, to please ask you. Be honest and let them know that your job is to leave them in a calm and pleasant state – you want to know, honestly, if you have succeeded. Hopefully, they will tell you they feel marvellous, better, more peaceful or uplifted. If they express any negative feelings, ask what may have prompted these and clear up the situation before your sitter leaves.

Taking responsibility for how you speak is crucial to making your sittings safe and enjoyable for all concerned. It is also an area of psychic work that can spill over into your everyday life and benefit your personal relationships. How often do we stop to think about what we are about to say before we say it – especially if we're angry, frustrated or excited? Start noticing how you speak at work and at home. When you rephrase certain remarks or stop to reflect on the power of your words before you speak, how does that change the way in which people respond?

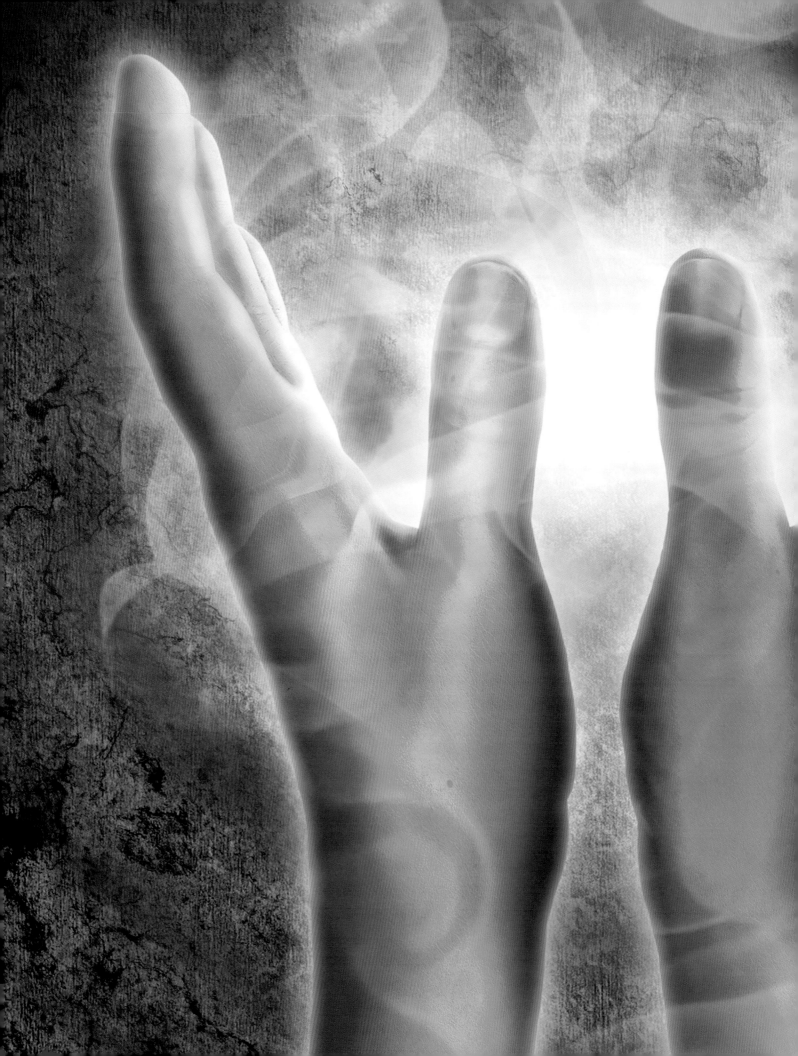

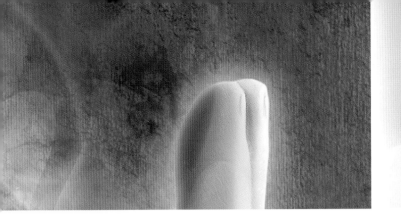

CHAPTER SEVEN:

Developing Your Powers

In this chapter we're going to look at auric reading, psychometry and flower clairsentience, and learn how to perform them safely and effectively. You will also be given the opportunity to better understand the aura, the power of inanimate objects and the beauty of flowers.

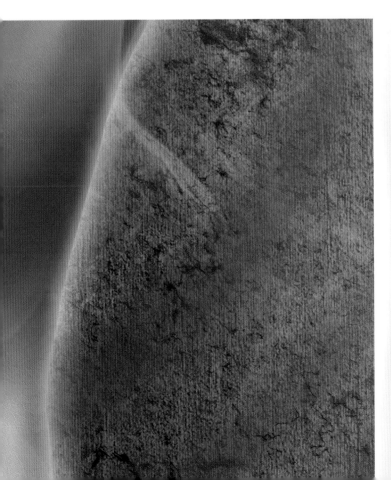

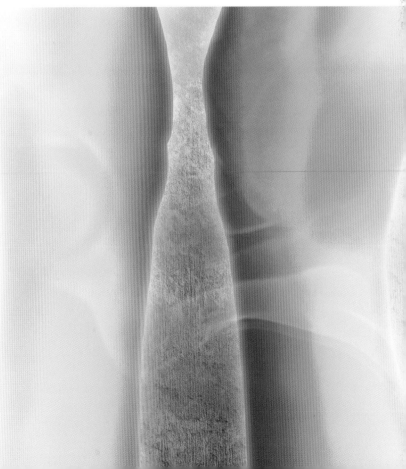

GIVING AN AURIC READING

When you have chosen your sitter – or, rather, when you have chosen each other – a good place for beginners to start is with an auric reading. This is when you tune in to someone's aura to get a reading of what is going on with that person in their present life, and it works on an emotional, feeling level. It helps if you understand that what you are doing in this process is tapping into your sitter's etheric level of the aura. This is the first layer of the aura and it deals with their present, physical life. An auric reading can provide wonderfully accurate details, but it can't tell the sitter something they don't already know, although it may tell them something from their subconscious as well as their conscious state. It involves you 'reading' the sitter from their aura and, because every aura changes constantly, what you receive will differ from day to day, even from hour to hour. Auric reading is a valuable starting point for psychics to learn how to work and test their accuracy.

AURIC LAYERS

The diagram of the seven levels of the aura (above) shows how each auric layer corresponds to a specific chakra. Remember that there are energy centre 'cones' of each chakra at each layer.

The auric layers are divided into three planes: physical, astral and spiritual. The physical plane refers to the first three levels and represents the etheric body (the first layer), the emotional body (the second layer) and the mental body (the third layer). These levels concern how we operate within our earth body and balance with our base chakra (physical), sacral chakra (emotional) and solar plexus chakra (mental).

Do you remember reading that our heart chakra is like a hinge linking our physical and spiritual beings? The astral plane refers to the fourth level, which is connected to our heart chakra. It is our bridge between the physical and spiritual worlds.

The spiritual plane refers to the fifth, sixth and seventh levels and is said to mirror the physical

plane. Level five mirrors the first layer, but in perfect, spiritual form; in other words, the fifth auric layer is the ultimate version of our first layer. Similarly, level six is the perfect mirror of our second layer and level seven is the perfect version of our third layer. You may have to read this paragraph a few times before it makes sense!

You will hopefully learn to work within the first three levels of the aura – the physical, emotional and mental – and tap into the energies within the physical plane. Tapping into someone's spiritual nature and higher consciousness takes dedication and practice. The closest you will get to touching upon the spiritual essence of a person at this stage will be by using flower clairsentience.

As we have seen, some people are easier to 'read' than others. You will understand this fully when you practise on different people. Some are more in touch with their spirituality than others. The more their energies vibrate within a certain level, the more likely you are to be able to tap into it. While there is a great deal you can learn about someone from their first three auric levels (their physical plane), you should always be aware that there is more than this to each person. Every human has seven layers of energy, whether they're aware of them or not.

If you have time before your sitter arrives, it helps to spend a while concentrating on the human aura. Think about its layers of information, remember the sensitivity of certain areas and consider how you will phrase delicate information. Go over the technique for expanding your own aura and be prepared to increase your auric field for this work.

When your sitter arrives, it's important to put them at their ease as much as possible. Hopefully you will have created a relaxing and inspiring space in which to work with them, and this should help! In this reading you are relying on the information within your sitter's aura and, as you now know, if you have someone who is nervous or frightened their aura will contract and make your work more difficult. Spend some time explaining what you're doing in a practical way and make every effort to relax them. Try to avoid asking personal questions during this time and, if your sitter offers details about themself, gently ask that they refrain from doing so until the end.

When you have helped them to relax as much as possible, explain that you'll take a few minutes to open up. Your sitter may feel awkward just sitting there as you do this, so you could encourage them to close their eyes and rest. If your sitter leads a hectic life, they may be more than happy to sit quietly. Make sure you let them know they don't have to do anything to help you, that they don't have to concentrate or try to project any image. The more relaxed they are, the less they try to do anything, the more it helps you. It's important you explain this clearly; people immediately feel better when told this. Any responsibility is taken from their shoulders and that's a comforting feeling.

Now you're ready to follow the exercise on the facing page.

EXERCISE — AURIC READING

Close your eyes and go through your opening-up process. Pay attention to expanding your own aura so that it feels more open. You may wish to ask the source of Universal energy to help you and thank it for its presence. When you feel open, balanced and relaxed, continue. You are now going to pull some of your sitter's aura into your own aura, so that you can read and interpret information about them. You don't have to keep your eyes closed for this, but it may help your concentration. Using your psychic lift, raise your energies up to your solar plexus chakra. Take a deep, comfortable breath and ensure that your energies stay at that level. As you breathe out, feel your aura expand and reach out into your sitter's auric field. Breathe in again and feel their aura being pulled back towards you. Breathe out and reach out with your aura again. Breathe in and feel their aura coming in. Repeat several times.

By doing this, you create an oval of constant energy reaching out to your sitter in an arc and returning to you in a second arc. You need to maintain this energy flow to keep receiving information. You can use different visualization techniques to help in this process. Imagine that your aura has a long arm that reaches out, scoops up your sitter's aura and returns it to you. Or imagine a brilliant, beautiful light that streams towards your sitter, mixes with their aura and then returns to you. As soon as you receive some information and speak, your energy will drop to your base chakra. You will need to lift your energies again, hold them at the solar plexus chakra and continue the cycle of energy. At this point you will appreciate how important it is to practise using your psychic lift on a daily basis. The more you have done this, the easier it will be when you have someone sitting in front of you.

During your reading it's likely you will pick up some uncomfortable sensations. Most people have aspects of themselves with which they're not content. Whenever you feel something unpleasant, stop the circle of energy flow and pull the white light down through your crown chakra, using it to cleanse and release anything unwelcome. Once you feel you have worked at a deep enough level with your sitter, let your energies settle back at your base. Cleanse thoroughly several times before you close down. Remember to retract your aura. Then cleanse again and check you're well earthed before you open your eyes. Now you can discuss with your sitter the information you have received.

INTERPRETING YOUR READING

Every psychic works differently and has to find
their own method of dealing with what they receive
psychically. Some people only get symbols or images;
others see only colours; some just feel and sense
emotions; others have physical responses only; some
may just hear music and songs! You may have a
jumbled mass of all the above until you can discipline
yourself. Most images and sensations will come and
go swiftly; some will tangle themselves into and
on top of each other and thus be hard to decipher.
Alternatively, you may feel and receive nothing.
This may mean that you are still feeling uncertain
about psychic phenomena or that auric reading isn't
a powerful medium for you. If this is the case, then
psychometry or healing may be a more suitable field
for your vibrations. Only through experimenting will
you know what works for you.

When you do get something, anything, say what
comes into your mind – always remembering your
responsibility to your sitter. Make sure you phrase
your words appropriately. What becomes difficult
now is preventing your brain from taking over and
interpreting everything for you. Provided the image
or sensation is not one that may worry your sitter,
say exactly what you see or sense. Do not decide for
yourself at this stage what it means.

For instance, if you see a body of water, tell your
sitter that you see a lake, sea or river, or whatever,
but don't immediately decide what that means.
Your brain might go on to say to you: 'They're going
to travel over water,' or 'They like boating,' but you
have to learn to shut out your thoughts. It's hard to
do. The truth is that water can relate to emotional
states, so the image you're seeing could be symbolic:
turbulent seas could mean a troubled mind, bubbling
whirlpools might indicate some confusion; a calm
lake might mean peace and joy in a present situation.
Only when you shut out your own thoughts and
interference will your reading be accurate.

Often your images may not make sense to you,
but they may make sense to your sitter, so say what

you see, however trite or nonsensical it seems. You might get a plate of baked beans on toast in front of your eyes and think you can't mention something so unimportant; but, if you did, you might discover your sitter had it for lunch! Find the confidence to say what you are getting and, if they can't relate to it, don't worry at this stage. It's wonderful just to be opening up and starting your psychic work, so don't expect too much immediately. Any time you receive something that is unpleasant or uncomfortable, immediately cleanse before renewing your energy and continuing.

The speed with which images come and go may be confusing at first. This is because you aren't keeping the cycle of energy flowing. Remember, as soon as you speak, the energy drops and so does the image. With practice, it becomes easier to keep the speech and energies working simultaneously.

Your sitter may not always connect a thought or image at the time you offer it, but it may make sense later. For example, you may see a little brown dog and ask if the sitter owns a dog. They may say

they've never owned a dog and don't even like them particularly! Then, later, they realize that on their bus journey over to see you a brown dog and his owner sat next to them for the whole journey. So what you saw was accurate because the little dog left some of his energies within your sitter's aura, even though the sitter was not aware of it.

Avoid trying to predict or offer solutions to problems you may pick up on. This is another common mistake made by inexperienced psychics. You may see, for example, that your sitter is about to take their driving test and is desperate to pass. You may 'see' them passing it, waving their certificate and smiling, so you say to them they will undoubtedly pass. You won't necessarily be right, because what you were picking up on in their aura was their intense desire to pass. They have created the image of passing because they hope for it so much. Predicting the future is not possible during an auric reading and, if you think you are doing so, you're probably only picking up on the sitter's desires.

CONCLUDING THE SESSION

As you run out of images or sensations, you will feel the energies weaken. Sometimes it's rather like the sensation of hitting ground level suddenly in a lift: a slight jolt as you return to earth. If you are using the visual image of your Sushumna being a psychic lift, you may indeed feel as though it has returned to ground level a little too swiftly! Always remember to cleanse as soon as you finish. Even as you ask the sitter for their response, practise flushing everything away with your psychic waterfall or pure white light. Keep doing it even as they're talking, provided you can concentrate on two things at once. Now ask them for as much feedback as you can. If you intend to do further sittings with them, don't encourage them to talk about situations and conditions unrelated to what you have mentioned; that way you'll have more to discover on a subsequent occasion. However, do discuss any images, colours or emotions that you picked up on earlier.

Some connections may make sense when you probe a little further. A colour you saw might simply be the colour their office or bedroom is painted. It's natural that this will be within their aura because they're surrounded by that colour for a large part of each day. You might have seen a sports car although they don't own a car themselves; perhaps that sports car belongs to a neighbour and is always parked outside, so they see it every morning as they leave home. Perhaps you got the image of a child's photo on a desk, but they say they've no photo on their desk either at home or at work. But they might sit opposite someone upon whose desk is a child's photo. Again, it will be an image firmly implanted in their subconscious and part of their aura.

When you first sit there, if nothing comes through quickly you might start to imagine that nothing will ever happen. You may worry that your sitter is fed-up or bored, which then might make you feel pressured into 'performing'. Unless you can cleanse that panic away and keep breathing and spiralling the energy, your brain will start to create things for you. After a few sessions you'll feel the difference for yourself when this happens and you'll be able to control it.

Conversely, when you do genuinely start reading someone's aura, your brain may raise nagging doubts that you must be imagining it and that you're not really capable of this work, and so on. Again, you have to cleanse those doubts and continue working. You must be in control at all times, so practise that feeling of containment from your very first sitting. Refuse to let your nerves and doubts take over; discover a new strength in yourself by doing so.

CLOSED SITTERS

You will find that some sitters are more closed than others. We all have our own protective shell that we need to go through life. Some people's shells are paper-thin, which makes it easier to work with them.

Others will have built up much thicker walls. You may occasionally work with someone who literally seems to have steel-plated armour all around them, together with a two-metre-thick brick wall! You then have a choice to make. You can try to help them open up a little by making an effort to relax them or you can try to tune in to them on an emotional level to see if you can gain some understanding as to why they seem so 'closed'. You then may have the opportunity to help them on a more personal level. Or you can honestly say to them that you aren't picking anything up, apologize and possibly offer them another reading on another day.

It is important to phrase your comments carefully. Find a positive way to discuss your sitter's apparent armour, if it feels appropriate, but be careful not to imply that this is problematic. Some people's jobs mean they have to develop strong self-protection because they work in potentially dangerous situations: police and mental health workers, for example. They need a protective cloak during working hours and they may unconsciously keep it on when they finish. For you to imply that they could open up more and drop their guard would be potentially hazardous for them.

You will also deal with people whose aura seems very uncomfortable to you. Not all people are happy and well-adjusted, and you will be able to sense this as you work with your sitters. This is when you need to practise your cleansing techniques and keep ridding yourself of unwanted images. You may find this becomes a real test for you, to keep cleansing and moving on until you find aspects of a person that you feel happy to discuss. Once you have given a sitting to someone you found to be more challenging than most, remember to cleanse thoroughly in your cleansing sanctuary and put an extra thick cloak of protection around yourself. Use your psychic pen to protect your chakras. Remember to finish your sitting on a positive note and make sure your sitter leaves in a good frame of mind.

PSYCHOMETRY

Once you have practised auric reading sufficiently to open up, control your energies, tune in and receive information, you can go on to try psychometry.

This is where you hold an object in your hand and tune in to its vibrations so that you can glean some of its history and, ultimately, an insight into the person to whom it belongs. In the case of inanimate objects, auric vibrations are determined by the living things that have surrounded and touched them. The term 'psychometry' was coined in 1842 by the eminent American physician and scientist J. Rhodes Buchanan (1814–99), who spent a large part of his life studying psychic phenomena. He fused the Greek words *psyche* (soul) and *metron* (measure) to produce psychometry, meaning 'soul measuring' or 'measurement by the human soul'. During psychometry your hands act as receptors for information, so wash them thoroughly and ensure your nails are trimmed and clean. You also want your hands to be as 'open' as possible, so try this simple exercise below.

EXERCISE – HAND BRUSHING

There are chakras in the palms of the hand and in the tips of the fingers. These need to be activated to heighten psychometric experiences. You can do this in a very straightforward way by rubbing your hands together briskly, palm to palm. It can be done lightly, rather than with force, but move your hands quickly for the best effect. Continue this brushing motion for about thirty seconds.

Now you are going to activate your fingertips. Place your left fingertips against your right and rub them briskly but lightly together. You can do this for a minute or so. As there is a wealth of meridians or energy lines at the tips of your fingers, you create a general sense of wellbeing as you do this. Notice which other areas of your body feel better for this experience. After this short exercise, you will have energized and sensitized your touching abilities.

THE RIGHT OBJECT

It is very important to choose the right object on which to practise psychometry. You don't want to make it complicated for yourself by having to deal with an object that has a mixture of vibrations from a combination of people. Ideally the object should have been close to someone for a period of time without outside influences. Keys and money aren't good choices, nor are objects that were previously owned by someone then passed down to the sitter, as you will get a mixed reading. Avoid stones and crystals, as they have strong vibrations of their own and may confuse you. Even something such as a watch that has been at the repairer's for a week recently could have the vibrations of the repair shop all over it. Imagine how confusing that could be with so many customers in and out of a shop. Be firm with your sitter about the object they want you to read and don't be afraid to ask questions if you're unsure.

Quite often a sitter may arrive with an object belonging to someone else, say a parent, who has recently passed over. They want you to tell them about their deceased parent. This isn't possible because a reading on the level you can give will only respond to the vibrations of that object. If their parent hasn't touched the object for a while, it will, in the meantime, have picked up other influences. Also, your sitter won't necessarily know who else has been close to that object before their parent. You see how complicated it can become? Be honest and explain that this is not the level at which you can work at present. To make contact with a deceased spirit requires your psychic lift moving very swiftly up to the top floors and needs a degree of discipline you haven't yet attained.

So what is a good object? If someone has been married for a while and bought their wedding ring new from a jeweller's, then that is an excellent choice. As it's also a symbol of their love for their partner, you will probably be able to pick up a fair amount about that relationship from it. Jewellery, in general, is a popular choice for psychometry because certain items may be worn permanently by people and are therefore heavily imbued with 'them' – but always check if the item is an antique and how long the person has owned it. A newish pen that only your sitter has used would also be filled with their vibrations. Likewise, an object they have made themselves would be suitable.

EXERCISE – PSYCHOMETRY READING

Psychometry requires the use of the chakras as far as the solar plexus, as in an auric reading. So again you need to settle yourself comfortably, open up all your energy centres, let the white light in through your crown and allow it to wash over you, and then lift your energies up as high as the solar plexus. It might be helpful if you also visualize the beautiful Universal energy sweeping strongly through your arms, hands and fingers, which will increase their sensitivity. Once you feel ready, ask your sitter to give you the object. Hold it loosely in one hand and remember to keep breathing and lifting those energies to the solar plexus. You may find through practice that one hand is more sensitive than the other, or you may like to use both by cupping the object. Try variations and feel the difference of each.

Give yourself plenty of time to receive the messages and images. Again, as with the auric reading, say exactly what you see and feel, always taking into account the suitability of what you are saying. You may find having a solid object in your hand gives you more confidence than trying to tap in to someone's aura. Use that confidence to express yourself clearly and always, as soon as you speak, remember to renew your energies.

Occasionally you will read an object and nothing you say will make any sense to your sitter. You need courage to keep going under those circumstances, but continue reporting what you see and feel for a few minutes and then, once they are sure they

can't take on board any of what you are saying, let the images go and cleanse yourself thoroughly. Then ask your sitter how long they have had the object and if they know who owned it before them. You will probably have tapped in to another owner whose personality was dominant, irrespective of how long ago they owned the object. Just as some people come across as more forceful than others, so objects respond accordingly. If your present sitter has a very contained energy and keeps their aura close to their physical body, it could explain why the previous owner is still dominating the object. Ask your sitter if they have another object they could give you and, if this isn't possible, perhaps offer them an auric reading so they don't feel they have wasted time being with you.

If you are working with a friend, and both of you try psychometry with the same object, you'll probably discover you each have a different reading to give on the same item. This is normal. One person may tap in to the sitter's emotional state and

the other may pick up material objects that surround the person. It is interesting if you can work with someone else to get used to the differences and know that each reading is valid, but from a different perspective.

Sometimes psychic work results in finding the complete opposite of something, especially in auric reading and psychometry. This is because people's dislikes create very strong emotions and those negative vibrations are easy to pick up on. You may see a cat, for instance, and say, 'You are very fond of cats. Do you own a cat?' Their response? 'Oh no, I hate cats. Can't stand them.' This may happen quite a bit, so if you aren't sure of the emotion attached to what you are seeing, you could always phrase it something like this, 'I see a cat around you very strongly. I think you must either love cats or have a fear of them.' Fear is another very strong emotion that has an effect on our aura and objects next to us. For example, if someone has a great fear of knives, you are quite likely to pick up on that in their aura. Again, think before you comment on an image like that. If in doubt, don't say anything about it but cleanse yourself and move on.

At the end, once you have handed the object back to your sitter, always remember to cleanse yourself thoroughly, paying particular attention to the Universal light sweeping down through your arms and hands and trickling out through your fingertips. If you have created a powerful cleansing sanctuary, make sure your hands are washed thoroughly in there.

PRACTISING PSYCHOMETRY ALONE

You can also practise psychometry on your own. The next time you receive a letter you don't recognize, pause before you open it. Hold it in your hands and do a mini 'reading'. What can you pick up? Or when you hear a 'ding' telling you that an email has come through, focus on who that email might be from before you check your inbox. If your mobile is ringing, think about who the caller might be before you answer it. After a bit of practice you will probably pick up some image and, if the letter, email or call is from someone you know well, you may even get a flash of their face in front of you.

Once you become aware of the aura that objects give out and start tapping in to their different energies, you acquire an even greater appreciation of how fascinating psychic work can be. Imagine what a visit to an antiques shop could be like for an experienced psychic – all those different objects holding a wealth of information and energies! Of course, an experienced medium knows how to shut themselves down tightly in such a situation: suddenly being bombarded by all that information at once would be impossible to handle.

FLOWER READING

Flower reading, also known as flower clairsentience or flower psychometry, is not as widely used as auric reading and psychometry, but it can be a very powerful way of 'reading' somebody. Your sitter holds a living flower for a brief while, then hands you the flower to 'read'. You use the flower's vibrations to tune in to your sitter. This might seem rather fanciful, but its unerring accuracy may amaze you. It's best if you have worked with auric reading and psychometry before you try flower reading, as the vibrations are slightly different. Whereas auric reading and psychometry generally deal with the 'here and now' of the person, flower reading goes to another level, taking the reader back to the sitter's early life; it also deals with their spiritual nature. You need to have worked with the other two types of reading to understand the difference.

For flower reading, you will use the heart chakra for the first time. The solar plexus and sacral chakras, which you have been using up to now, are the feeling, emotional centres of the physical body, so you have been tapping in to people very much on that level. Now, using the heart chakra, you are starting to work in a slightly different area, becoming aware of subtler vibrations. With flower reading, the heart chakra helps you to tap in to the deeper spiritual needs of a person. You move past the etheric level of their aura and into further layers that are finer and lighter.

You can use any type of flower provided it's

fresh, not dried or artificial, and has a stem at least 3in (7.5cm) long. Your sitter should preferably be the only person to handle it before they pass it to you. If someone else has to hold it during this process, they should only handle it through another substance, such as paper. The ideal would be for your sitter to pick a flower of choice from their own garden, as different flowers reveal different aspects of a person. A thick-stemmed, heavy flower shows the stronger nature they present to the world, while a soft, wispy flower tells you about their inner emotions. If your sitter chooses their own flower it means they are also choosing, albeit subconsciously, that aspect of their personality they will benefit from looking at. Of course, not everyone has a garden; if this is the case, it's best if your sitter chooses a flower from a florist's or a friend's garden.

Your sitter needs only to hold the flower for a short while before they hand it to you. While they're holding it, they don't need to concentrate or think of anything in particular. Offer them a cup of tea or coffee and have a chat or just relax! Let them run their hands up and down the stem and lightly over the flower head. This isn't an exercise on thought transference: the flower's vibrations work on a much subtler, more spiritual level than that.

Once you have finished, ask your sitter for feedback. It's best to start with the bits they couldn't understand. Check to make sure it wasn't your phraseology or incorrect interpretation of something that was confusing. Even at this stage, it will be hard for you not to let your brain interfere on certain levels. As a beginner, you will find that there are always some inaccuracies; 'opposites' will crop up, when you interpret a dislike of something as a love of it, for example. Conversely, you may find the medium of flower reading to be one of the most accurate forms of psychometry.

Some people find flower reading uninspiring. If you're one of them, don't worry, but do try it with more than one person and preferably with different types of flower before deciding it isn't for you.

Connecting with flower energies can help strengthen your understanding of reincarnation and karma. Think of a seed as being a person's soul that grows into a physical entity before eventually dying. Yet the spirit of that entity didn't really 'die' because the flower's seed can then be used to create its next life. Our souls are our spiritual seeds that never die, but are reborn into new bodies. The karmic effect relates to how we look after ourselves in a lifetime: do we nurture, nourish and protect our souls from bad weather and outside influences, keeping ourselves as strong as we can, so that our souls learn, adapt and flourish, taking that essence forward into the seed which becomes our next life?

EXERCISE – FLOWER READING

While your sitter is making contact with the flower, you can concentrate on the opening-up process, making sure you feel comfortable and ready to work. Remember you have to draw the energies up to the heart centre now and it may take you a little longer to do that. The more you have practised moving your energies up and down in your psychic lift, the easier this will be.

When you're both ready, have your sitter hand you the flower. Hold it lightly in your hands, close your eyes and start feeling its vibrations from the base of the stem. The base represents your sitter's early life, from birth. As you work your way up the stem, you travel through their life to the present, which is the head of the flower. This reveals most about the spiritual nature of your sitter. It means a variety of things – their spiritual needs, their aspirations, the path they are meant to tread in life. Slowly work your way up the stem. You don't need to rush this process, but don't stop to dwell on a particular aspect for a long time. The smoother your journey up the flower, the easier it will be for you to keep a flow of contact and conversation. For this reason, ask your sitter to remain silent until you have finished the reading.

Every time you speak, remember to renew your energies up to your heart again. You may keep lifting only to your solar plexus to begin with, as this is all you have known until now. If that happens, let the energy drop again straightaway and then take another breath and lift up as far as the heart. It may take you a while to master this next level.

Speak as soon as you sense something. You may see flashes of your sitter as a baby, or objects that meant something to them in their youth, or feel strong emotions relating to their childhood. Even as you feel the sensations, keep moving slowly up the stem. You will probably find messages coming to you more quickly at this stage. The reason is that your sitter's energies are moving on to a faster dimension, because the flower's vibrations are speeding them up. This is why flower reading can be a powerful and accurate form of psychometry.

As you work your way up the flower, try to give a rough idea of the sitter's age when you comment on

periods of their life, otherwise they may be confused. You don't need to open your eyes to see how far up the stem you are to calculate the years. You may see the sitter in your mind and know their age that way, or see the number in front of your eyes, or you may just 'know' the approximate age they were at that time. You may sense periods of their life that don't yield any information for you, perhaps because your sitter chooses not to look at that part of their life. Don't dwell on anything unpleasant or upsetting. If you instinctively feel it is beneficial to pass comment, such as – 'You went through a difficult period in your late twenties, but you have learnt from it and become stronger as a result' – that is fine. Negative comments should always have a positive balance. Cleanse constantly if you pick up uncomfortable feelings and then lift your energies up to the heart again.

As you reach the head of the flower, you will probably have stronger emotional and spiritual reactions. Sometimes, as you touch the head of the flower, it can be like an explosion of feeling or understanding. On this level, use your heart as well as your solar plexus and sacral chakras to give a deeper reading. Until you experience this for yourself, it's hard to describe it. You will say something because you 'know' it, not because someone has told you or because you see it clearly in your head. You're working on a finer vibration and once you experience it, you will always be able to tell the difference. As you linger over the head of the flower, you may find yourself saying things you never expected to say, on a level of understanding you hadn't been aware of before. You may see more symbols than usual, but this time you will be able to clarify their meaning, whereas before you weren't certain. You will see deeper into the core of a person's spirituality on this level without it being an effort. At this stage, you will probably know when the reading is over as you will feel your energies suddenly drop of their own accord. Always try to finish a reading with something positive and encouraging for your sitter.

Take a moment to cleanse yourself and renew your energies before you open your eyes again. Focus on an object to ground yourself or use the image of your feet with roots attached to them, growing deep into the ground. You've been working on a higher vibration and it may take you an extra minute to come back down to earth so that you can focus properly on your sitter. You may find your own emotions came closer to the surface during this reading because of lifting your energy to the heart chakra. Make sure you wash away anything personal.

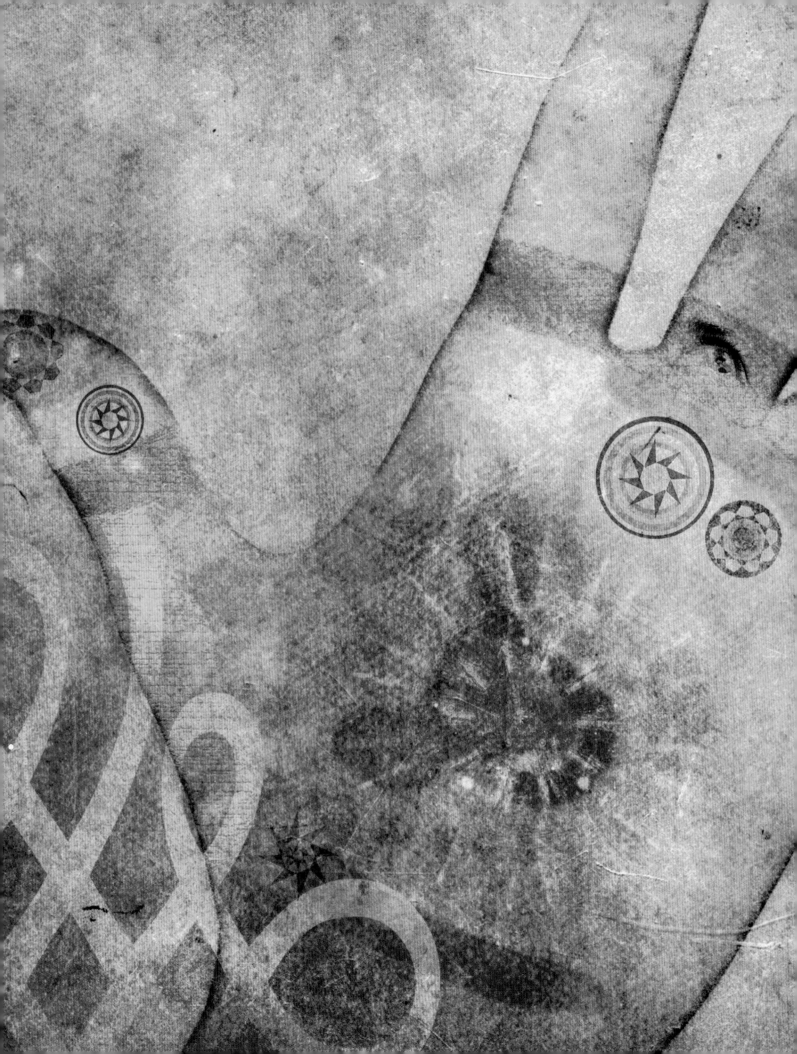

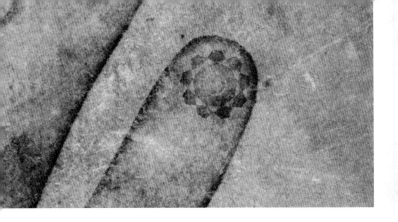

CHAPTER EIGHT:

Your Progression

In this final chapter, we are going to discuss further techniques to strengthen your connection with your inner psychic and look at additional methods you can adopt to protect yourself. We're also going to consider options for moving forward and developing yourself further.

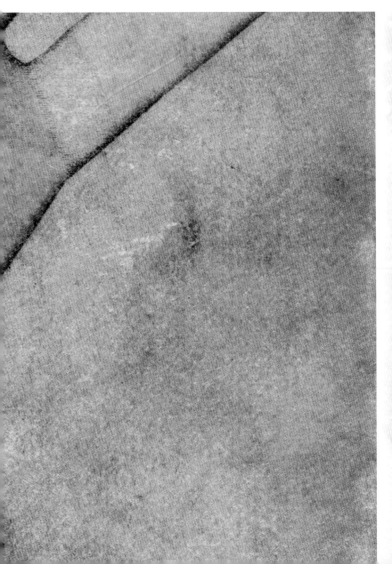
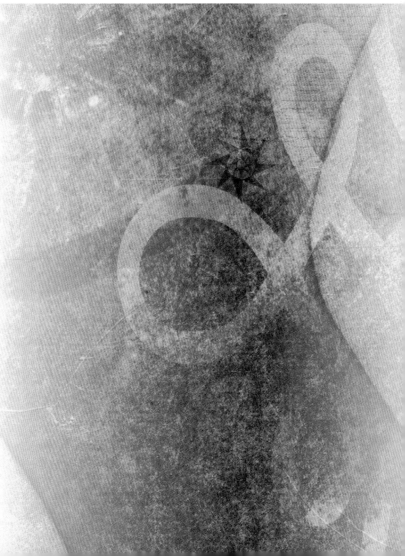

BLOCKS AND DIFFICULTIES

Working with so many energies is a confusing business and, as you progress in your psychic work, various problems will crop up that you'll find frustrating. But they are all part of your growth and necessary for your learning process. Some days you'll feel as though you are literally flying: your readings will have a high degree of accuracy and sitters will feel the benefit of what you have offered.

Other days will find you grumpy and insecure about your abilities: you'll receive little or no information and your sitters won't understand any of the scant information you do receive. There are several reasons for these blocks, so here are a few possibilities for you to consider.

CHECKING YOUR PERSONAL SPACE

First, look at the room in which you are working. What you created initially as your personal space may have felt right in the beginning, but as you change and grow, so your space may need to change. Do the colours inspire you now? What about the pictures? How are your plants looking? How often do you use candles, music or incense? How clean is your space? How tidy is it? When was the last time you clapped your hands around the space to clear any dead energy? Your space can become 'stale' if you don't keep tuning in to it and re-energizing it.

CHECKING YOURSELF

Secondly, be honest with yourself. How much are you following through with what you know is important in your lifestyle? How well are you sleeping, eating and exercising? How often do you find at least fifteen minutes to yourself to practise? Is it every day? How much water are you drinking every day? What focus are you giving to the clothes and colours you wear and how they make you feel? None of us is perfect and we can all slip up and fall back into bad habits. If you know you are doing this, resolve to change at least one aspect and stick to it.

CHECKING YOUR CHAKRAS

As you go through your opening-up process, you may find that one chakra is more difficult to open than another, either because you can't seem to visualize the colour properly or because it simply won't open for you. There can be a variety of reasons for this, and only you will be able to work out what is going on.

Of course, the ideal is to cleanse those conditions away as you work, so go back to your pure white light and the waterfall and cleanse through before trying to open further. Even on good days you'll find it's easier to open some chakras than others, just as some colours may be easier for you to visualize than others. Continual practice will enable you to improve, but when you hit a block on a particular energy centre remember to be kind to yourself. The more you push anxiously to try to clear the block, the more you will hinder yourself. Instead take a quiet moment to tune in to yourself to see what feels wrong, then cleanse again.

If, through spending time opening and closing your chakras, you sense that one is particularly closed or dysfunctional and you aren't managing to clear it, make sure you find some quiet time to focus on that chakra and work out the root cause of the discomfort. To do so, go back to the original exercises where you focused on your chakras in Chapter Two. Use everything you now know about that chakra to focus on it: colour, Sanskrit name, element, action and animal associated with it. Remember that different types of music will activate different chakras. Allow yourself to become totally immersed in the chakra so that you feel you actually ARE that energy centre. Work with any information you receive as a result to clear the block. You may find connecting with your Hara, as in the exercise on page 70, can also help your understanding.

By now you should have a powerful cleansing and closing-down process that you use, so when you need to let go of any experiences within that chakra and return to the 'real' world, you should be well equipped to do so.

YOUR PERSONAL PROGRESS

Another block may occur if you are working with somebody else, or if you are reading various books on psychic work, and it suddenly seems as if nobody is doing things the same way as you. This may make you feel uncomfortable and insecure. Our natural instinct is to want to follow the herd and when we find ourselves being pointed in a different direction it can be very disconcerting. But all psychics work differently and however you are developing is right for you. Don't compare or compete with others,

but be proud to be individual in your growth. No two auras are alike, so why should people be? Embracing your unique talents will clear other blocks in you.

Another common problem is that you rarely progress at an even rate in psychic work. You may stay at the same level for a long time, then move forward rapidly, only to stop suddenly again and not progress further for ages. It can be very frustrating, but this is natural, as you can only move forward to another level when you are ready. The frustration comes when you are certain you are ready, but still nothing shifts. Again, the more you push against this, the longer it will take you to move on. Accept each level you are on, and know you will move forward when you are ready.

CHECKING YOUR SITTER'S ENERGY

If you have an unsuccessful sitting (everyone has one occasionally, even experienced psychics) look to the points mentioned above and, if none of those seems to apply, then (and only then) think about your sitter. Did they want to come or were they coerced? Were they closed to the psychic experience and uninterested in what you had to say? Did they say

'no' to everything, almost before you had finished a sentence? Were they nervous about the experience and not able to relax at all? There will always be people who are cynical about psychic work, as well as those who are frightened of it, and such emotions make it hard for you to work successfully.

See this as a good 'test' for yourself and do your best to alleviate their fear and insecurities by explaining the basics of psychic work so that you eliminate the 'voodoo' element of it. Try using a very simple analogy to explain something such as auric reading to them. For instance, you could say: 'Your aura is like a homemade movie of your life. All I'm doing in reading your aura is borrowing your movie and running it through my projector, which is my mind.' They may not completely understand you, but it may reassure them. Once you have done a few sittings, you will work out for yourself what is going on and how best to handle each sitter.

BE KIND TO YOURSELF!

The more you develop your psychic gifts, the more you may notice changes in yourself – and not always for the better. As you become increasingly sensitive

You are developing an appreciation of human, Earth and Universal energies, how they work and how powerful they are.

to energies around you, you may find yourself less on an even keel emotionally and physically. That's why you must be gentle with yourself, especially initially. You are developing an appreciation of human, Earth and Universal energies, how they work and how powerful they are. It's wonderful to discover, but it has drawbacks. In addition to struggling with your own discipline and energies, you are being bombarded by other people's! This can make you more emotional than usual and you may feel disorientated and generally out of sorts at times. Places you once frequented may start to feel uncomfortable. As your awareness increases on a psychic level, so your hearing becomes more acute. Loud music and raucous voices may disturb you when once you could ignore them. It may also take less alcohol for you to feel inebriated. If, for example, you work in a hospital or environment with people who are not always in good health this may start to affect you more than usual.

If this happens, you need to keep closing down all through the day to keep those emotions in check. The solar plexus, in particular, is a strong centre that we tend to open without realizing. Use your psychic cloak of protection whenever you need it. Protect your chakras with your psychic pen. You have the comfort of knowing that no one else is aware of what you are thinking or doing, so you can repeat the processes as often as you like. If at any time you feel you are being attacked by unpleasant energies or emotions, there are additional measures you can take to protect yourself. Hopefully, many of you will never need to use these methods as you will be going around so well closed down and wrapped up that nothing unwanted can creep through. However, if you are feeling vulnerable and surrounded by difficult influences, there are some extra steps you can take in the exercises on pages 124–5.

EXERCISES – CREATING SOME EXTRA DEFENCES

THE MIRROR

You may be with somebody who is behaving aggressively or threateningly towards you. Perhaps you would usually laugh it off or otherwise deflect the situation, but today you feel vulnerable. Instead of reacting angrily yourself, hold an imaginary mirror up to this person so that their anger is directed back at them. You don't literally need to lift your arms and mime a mirror – your thought process alone is powerful enough for the person to have a subconscious reaction. Their anger may either stop or fizzle out, or they may just take a step backwards, but they won't know that you have done anything to bring about their sudden cessation in feeling.

CLOSED BODY LANGUAGE

If you are in a situation where you feel uncomfortable and want a quick means of protecting yourself (in addition to your personal psychic cloak), you can try simply folding your arms across your solar plexus (a very vulnerable chakra) and crossing your ankles. It immediately closes you off from people in a physical way.

YOUR SHINY DUSTBIN

Would you like to feel invisible? Imagine jumping into a brand-new, gleaming dustbin and shutting the lid on top of yourself. (Always imagine the bin clean and shiny so you don't pick up unhealthy energies.) If you find this a claustrophobic image, just choose another one.

YOUR CRYSTAL

Placing yourself within a clear crystal can also be helpful. Create a beautiful, strong crystal and put yourself in the centre of it. You can still see out, but people can't touch you.

YOUR BUBBLE

If that image still seems too restricting, pop yourself into a clear bubble. Create an imaginary filter screen all around you which allows you to breathe freely and participate in everything, but which filters out unhappy and unpleasant vibrations.

SEND LOVING ENERGY

Another very powerful way of dealing with someone who is giving you a hard time is to send out beams of love and light from your heart and solar plexus. Just as you have learnt to reach out with your aura to tap in to someone else's, so you can send out streams of love to calm someone else's upset emotions. It takes strength on your part to do it, when all you may feel like returning is a dose of your own anger, but once you feel the benefits of doing it, the action becomes easier to repeat. If colour helps you to visualize the process, use streams of green light going from your aura towards the other person. Remember not to let yourself receive anything back energetically from them – this is important. You are in control of choosing to give something from your own energetic field and you decide how much to give and when to stop the flow. If you are someone who opens up very easily and gets very affected by others' emotions, you might not want to use this technique.

PROTECTIVE SYMBOLS

There are lots of symbols used for protection and you might find one that feels right for you to wear around your neck or keep in your pocket. Depending upon your beliefs, you might want to consider a cross, a Star of David or a crescent moon. Look at images such as the Eye of Horus, the ankh or the yin/yang symbol and see if any of these appeal to you.

EXERCISES – LIFTING YOUR ENERGY

Of course there will be times when you simply want to refresh your energy or make it lighter and brighter! Far from feeling that you want to close yourself off energetically, perhaps you would like to feel even better connected with everything around you.

THINK HAPPY

If you are in a situation that has left you low in energy, a simple way to improve your energy is to think of something that makes you feel immediately happy – it could be a living being such as your child or pet, or an object that makes you feel good, or a beautiful setting such as a sunset, rainbow or seascape.

THERAPEUTIC MUSIC

Music can be a great healer of troubled emotions or simply lift you up when you want more energy! You will need to spend some time tuning in to different types of music to find what affects you the most, as once you start developing your inner psychic, your musical tastes may change a little. When you find something you particularly like, notice which chakras in your body are most energized. Are those the chakras you find more challenging (or easier) to open?

CLEANSING YOUR SPACE

If you feel your personal space could use a little energetic uplifting, try lighting some candles, using a 'smudge stick', or burning an aromatherapy oil to cleanse and freshen the room. Eucalyptus, juniper, pine and peppermint are good for clearing negative energies and marjoram is excellent for calming if you feel you have taken too much on board psychically. There are oils that can help enhance spiritual awareness,

One last thought: each of us is under increasing pressure today, at work and at home, to be the most efficient, the fastest, the very best at everything we do. We often forget just to stop and relax. Even if you can only find five minutes a day, try to give yourself that time to sit down, concentrate on your breathing and use your waterfall and light to cleanse and refresh yourself.

such as clary sage, basil and frankincense. As mentioned earlier, check with your health practitioner about any medical conditions that make using certain oils inadvisable.

HELPFUL CRYSTALS

You may be someone who responds well to stones and crystals, which are often used to increase psychic awareness. You may have been experimenting already with a few in your personal space, but if not then you might want to consider some of the following:

- amber is good for purifying and drawing out negative energies
- jet is helpful for shielding you from negative thoughts
- tiger's eye is renowned for its spiritual protection
- rose quartz is used to encourage a state of unconditional love.

Additionally, stones that are the colour of your chakra can help you to connect better with each energy centre. For example, you could use red jasper for the base, carnelian for the sacral, citrine for the solar plexus, malachite for the heart, blue turquoise for the throat, lapis lazuli for the third eye and amethyst for the crown. These are only suggestions; if you want to work further with crystal energies, spend some time in a crystal shop and absorb the energies of the different stones to see which you are drawn to.

If you do decide to use crystals and have them in your personal space, make sure you cleanse them frequently because they absorb the energy around them. You can do this by holding them under running water for a few minutes or leaving them in bright sunlight for a few hours. You can cleanse jewellery and other items by these methods, too.

LOOKING AHEAD

This book won't enable you to instantly access your inner psychic, but you can use it to develop a basic understanding and gradually increase your awareness and your gifts. If reading it has made you want to learn more and develop your skills, then you can do so in a variety of ways.

First, read anything and everything about subjects relating to psychic and holistic matters.

Attend as many lectures, workshops, weekend seminars, spiritual fairs, festivals and retreats as you possibly can. No one should ever tell you that psychic work only operates in one way and under a certain set of guidelines. It is such a complex subject that you can approach it from many different angles and decide for yourself what suits you best.

Don't limit yourself just to psychic phenomena. As the psychic operates very much in the spiritual and holistic realm, look into other related subjects, for example, colour therapy, crystals, aromatherapy, homeopathy, holistic massage, acupuncture, Alexander technique, meditation, Kirlian photography, yoga, feng shui, astrology, theosophy, graphology, numerology, tai chi, astral travel, qigong, dowsing and reiki. Look in health and New Age shops, browsing the bookshelves and studying new products on offer. Start discussing the concepts of spirituality/karma/reincarnation with friends and relatives. You'll probably be amazed that people you thought completely unconnected with psychic work have had an interest for quite a while. A fascinating aspect of psychic work is that once you open your mind to other possibilities, you seem to attract like-minded people to you.

However, the best way to improve your psychic abilities is to join a development circle. This is a mutually supportive group of novice psychics, run by an experienced psychic. You can progress further under guided tuition because you will feel safe, supported and nurtured. How can you find such a circle? There are a growing number of psychic and spiritualist organizations around the world and if you contact any one of them they will let you know whether they can offer a place. Always meet the teacher before committing yourself and use your tuning-in process to see if you feel comfortable with them and the organization to which they belong. If you can find the appropriate group for you, there

is no other single, more powerful choice you could make to improve your psychic development.

If you found this book interesting but are uncertain about its content, then it will still have benefited you in some way, as you are likely to find yourself being more aware of other people and atmospheres around you. You may not consciously realize this, but those close to you will sense a difference and this increased awareness can only benefit yourself and others.

As humans, we are more complicated – and more wonderful! – than we generally acknowledge. This book is intended for all of you who feel that way instinctively, but rarely take the time to think about it in greater depth. Enjoy your psychic and spiritual growth, and may you feel guided, protected and blessed on each step of your journey.